I am grateful to God for everything! And I believe that the meaning of life is to give meaning to other lives. A.M., you are the meaning of my life.
Lov U

Vinicius Borges
2024

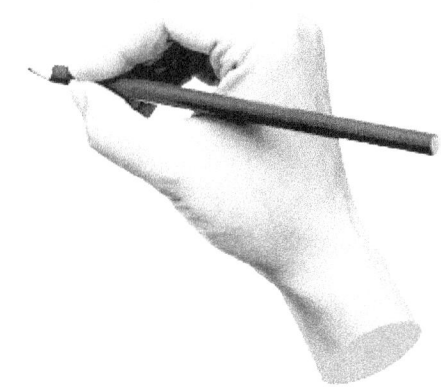

This Book Belongs to:

○━━━━━━━━━━━━━━━━━━━━━━━━━━━○

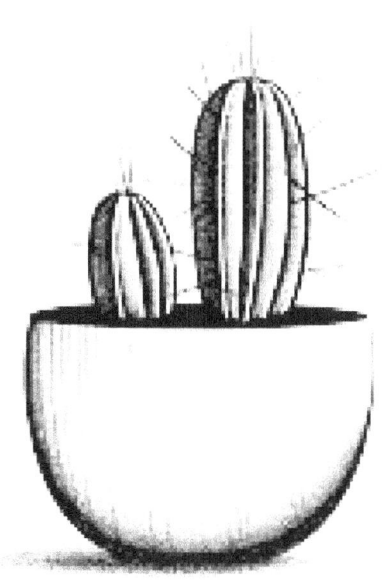

Test Color Page

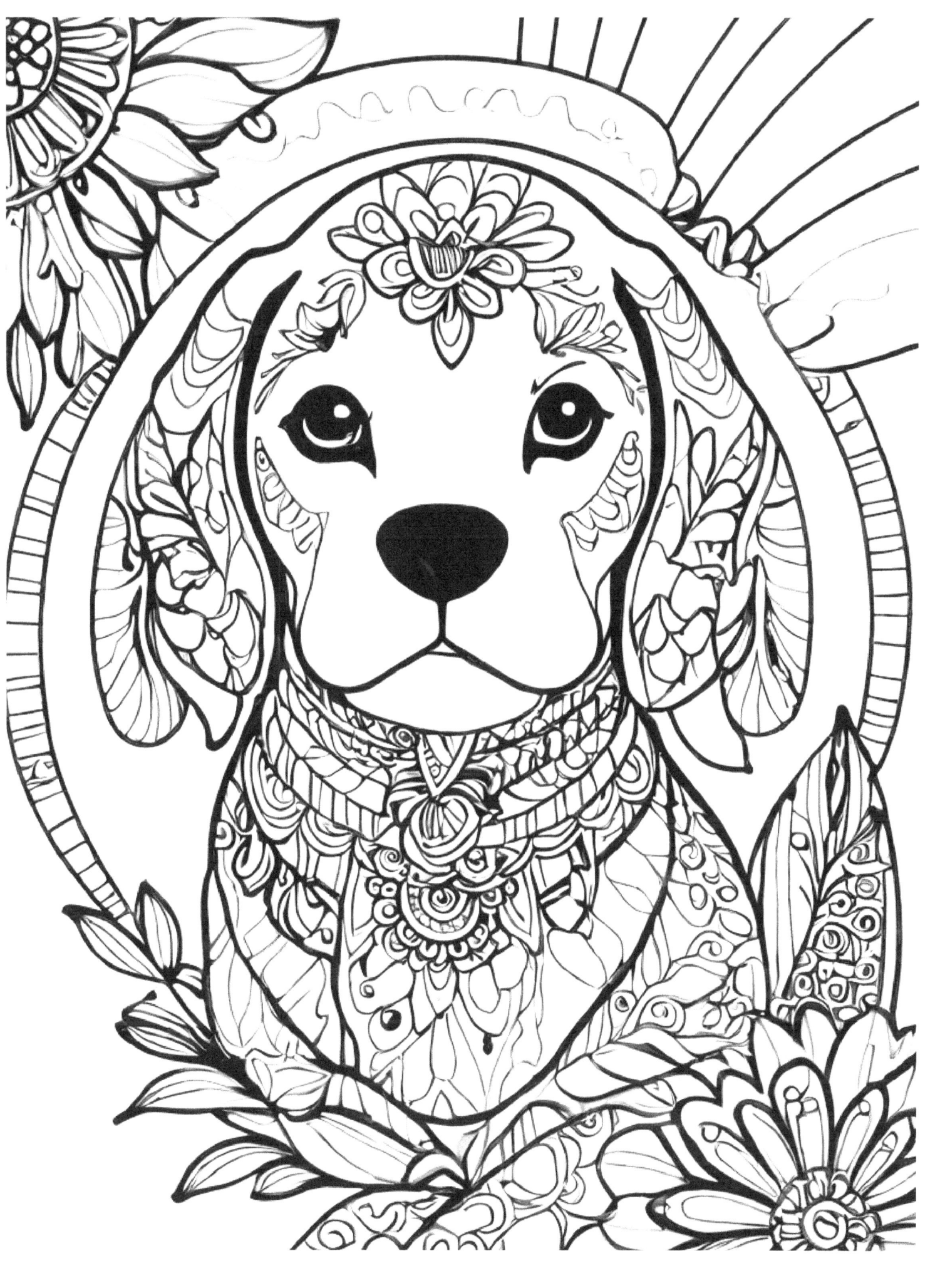

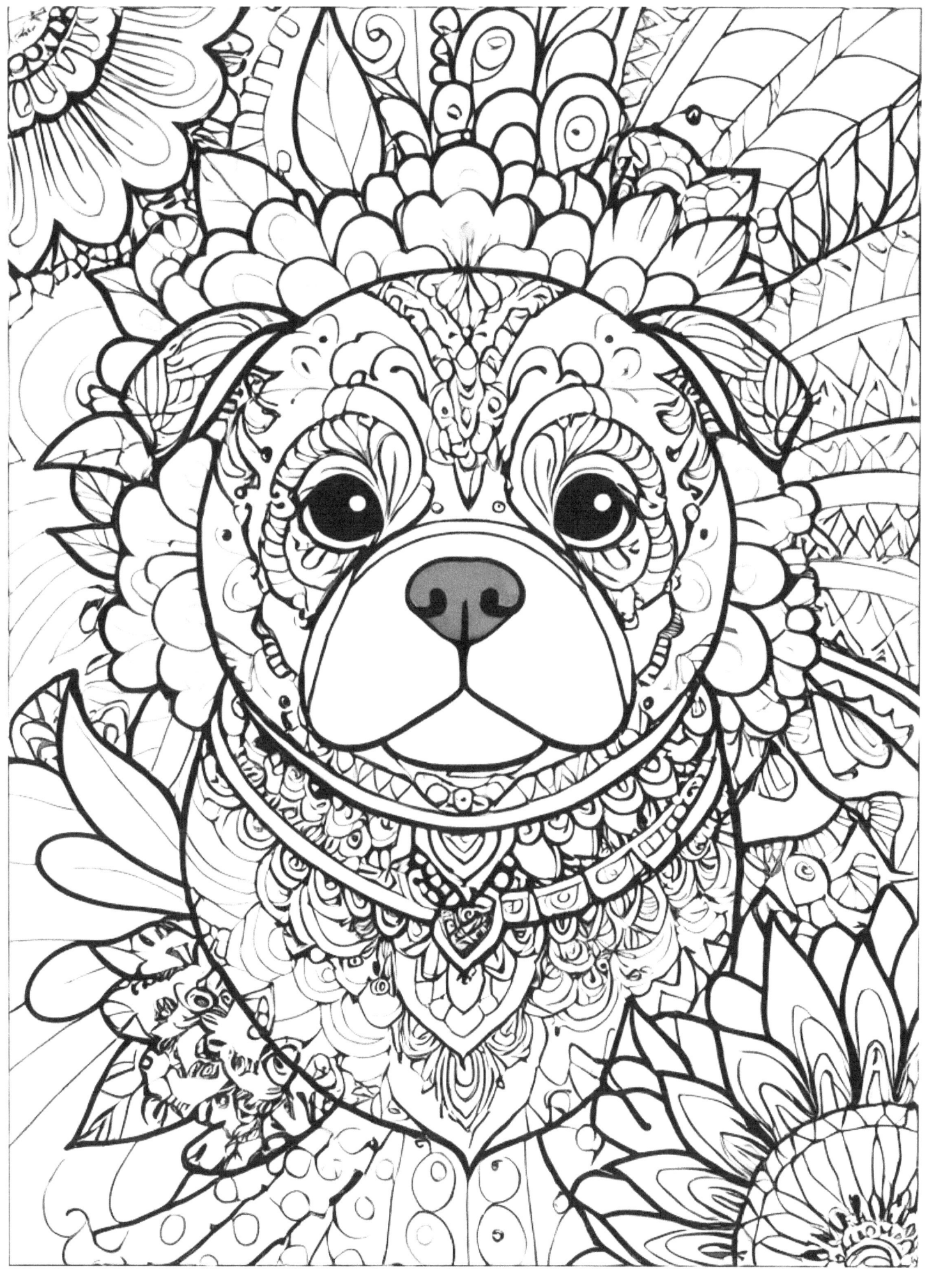

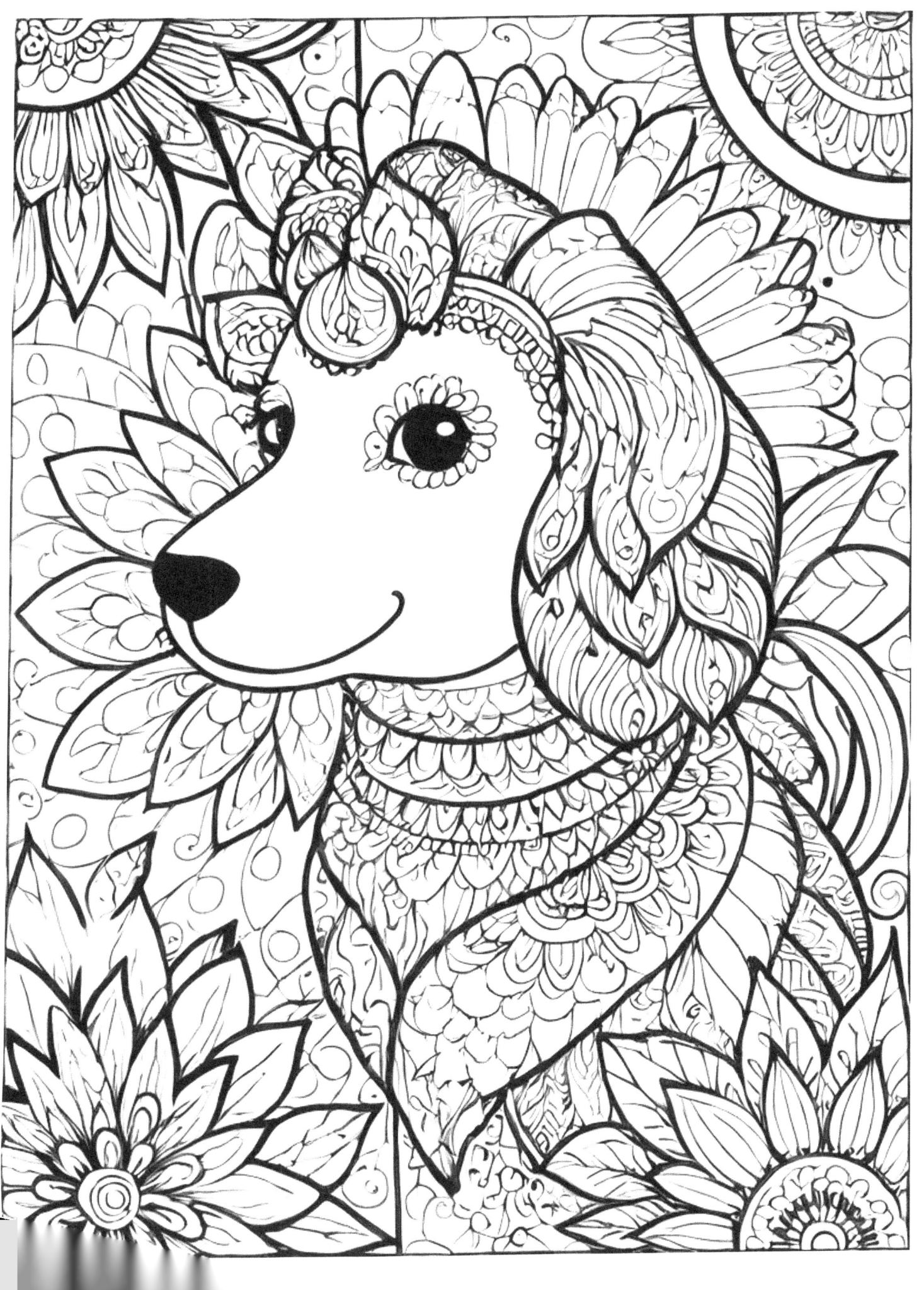

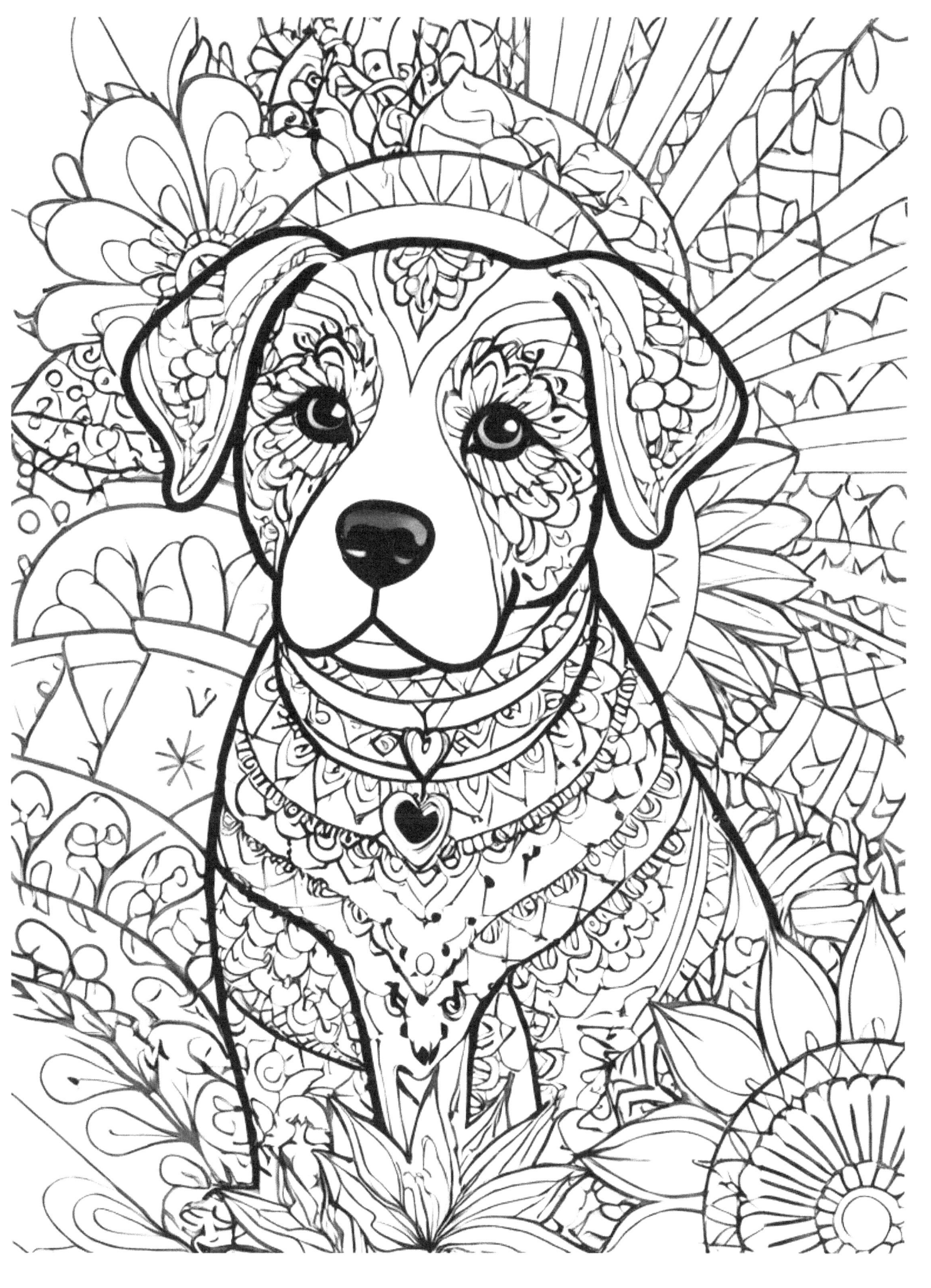

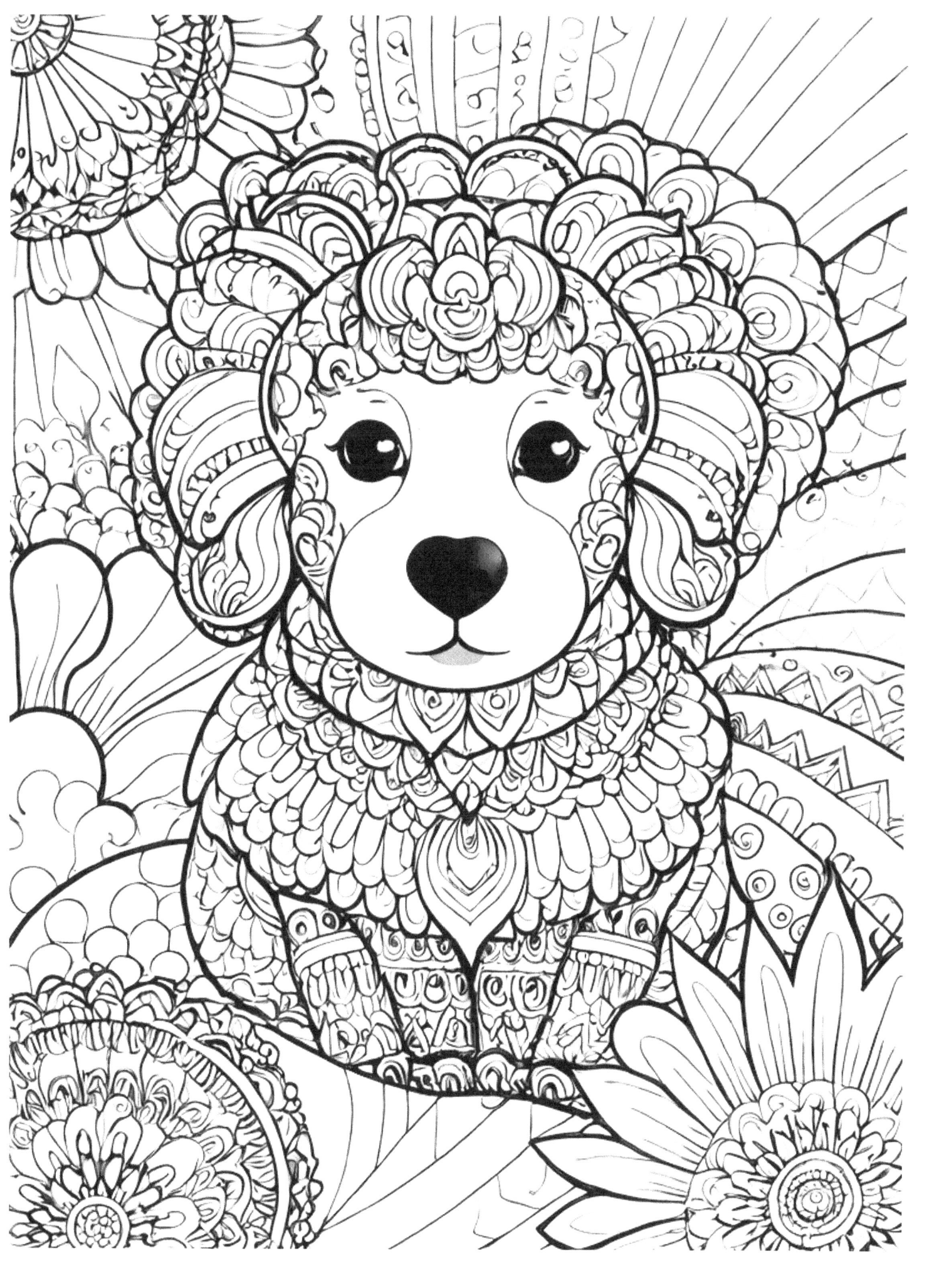

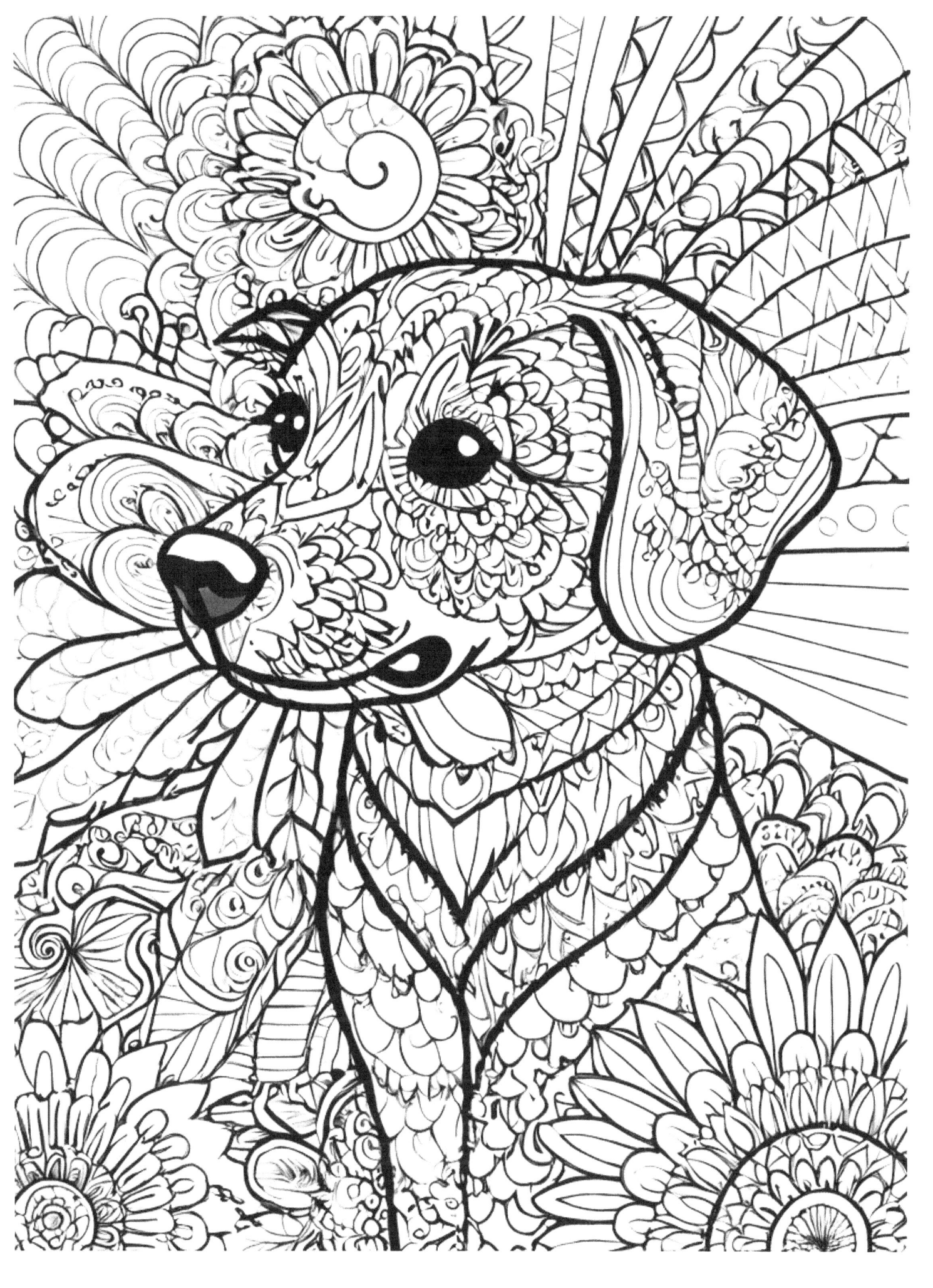

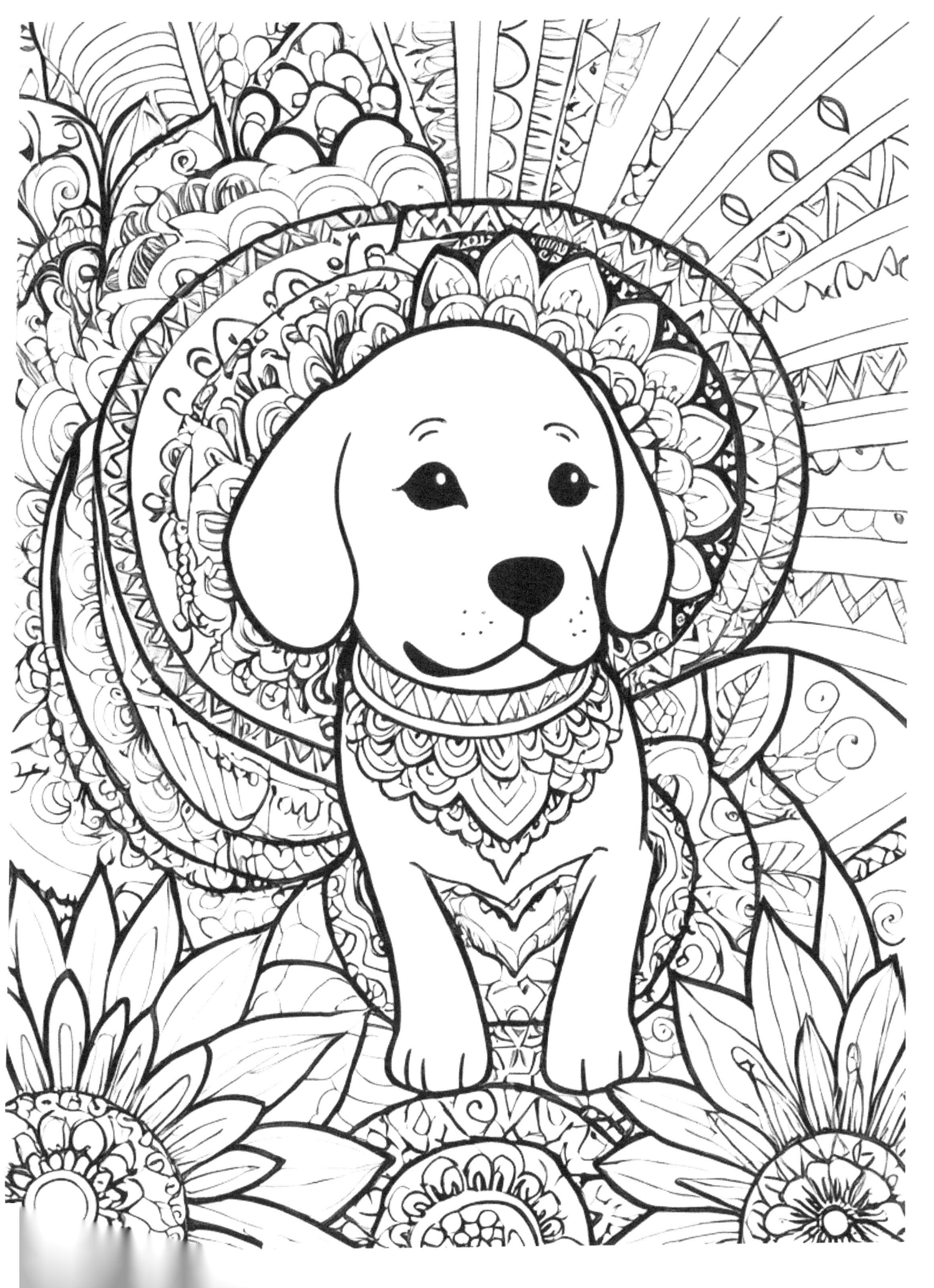

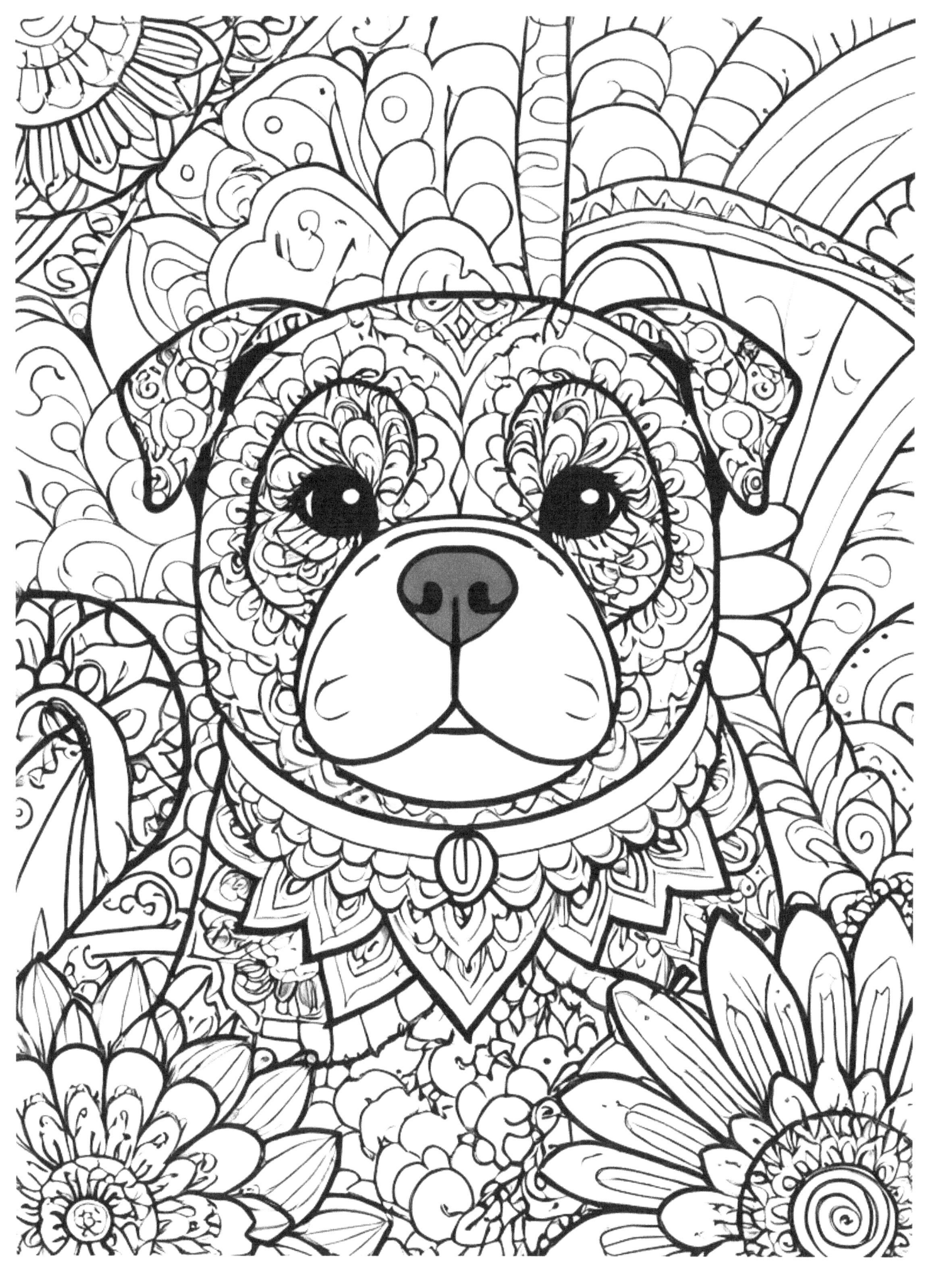

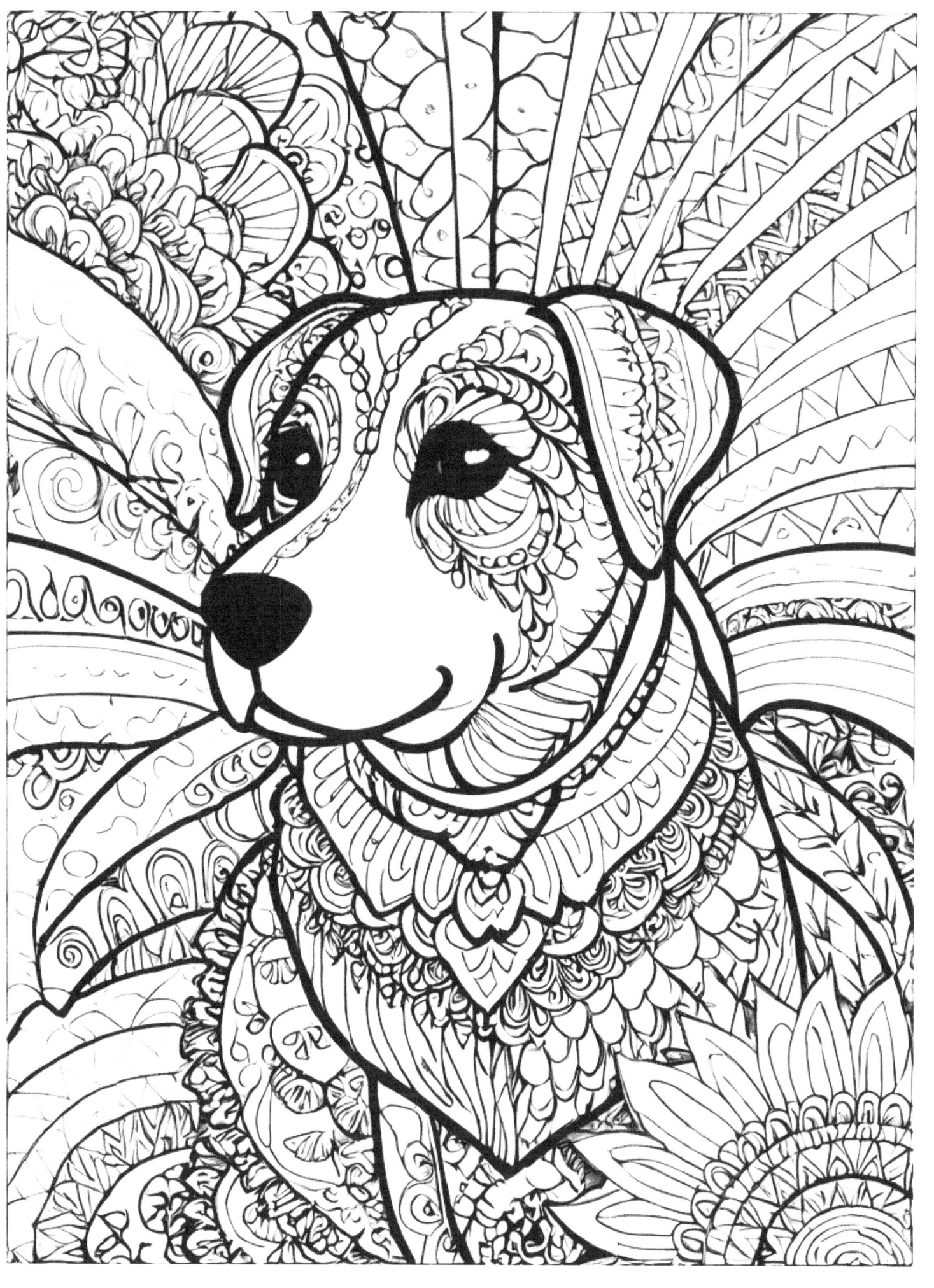

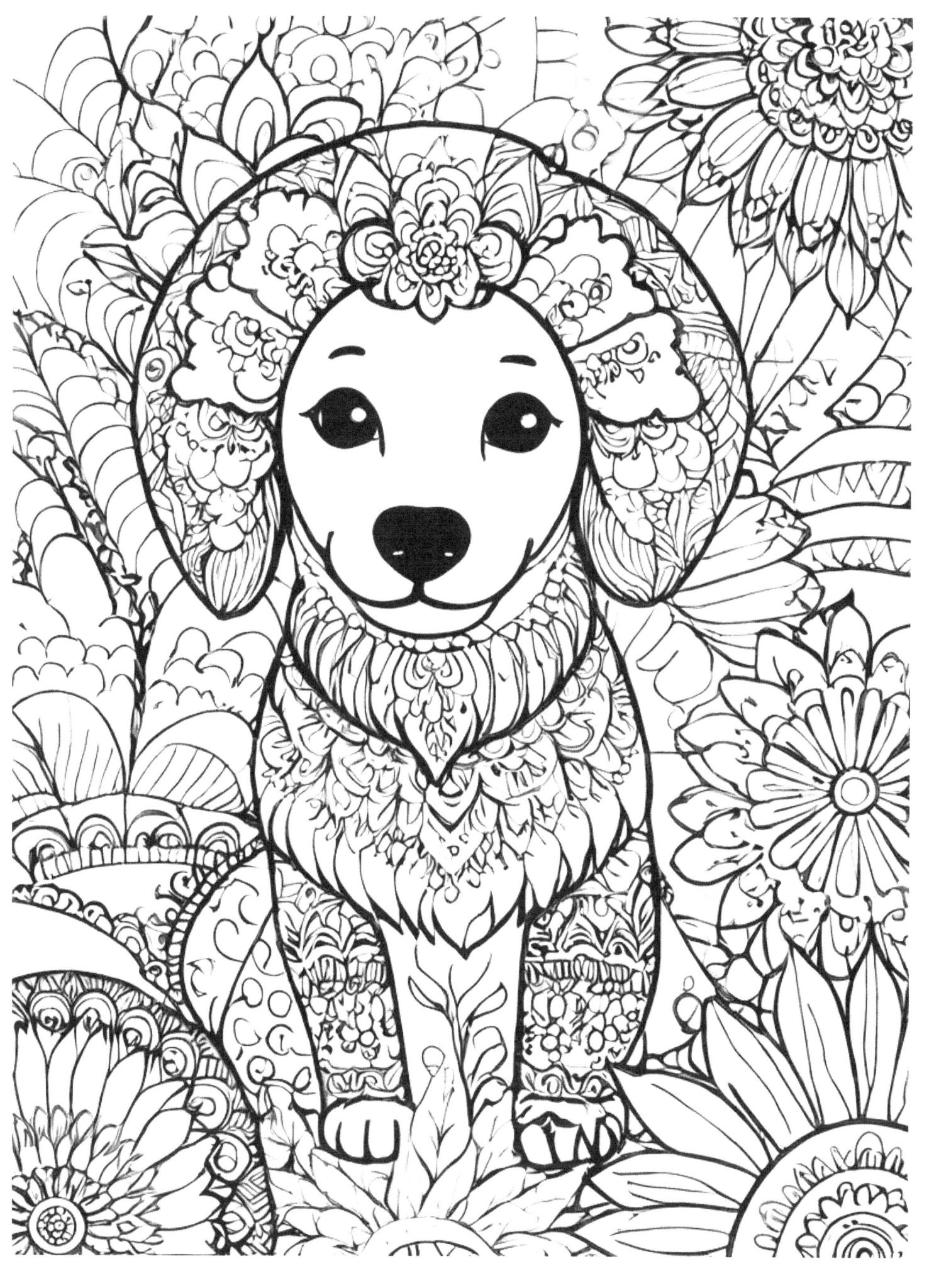

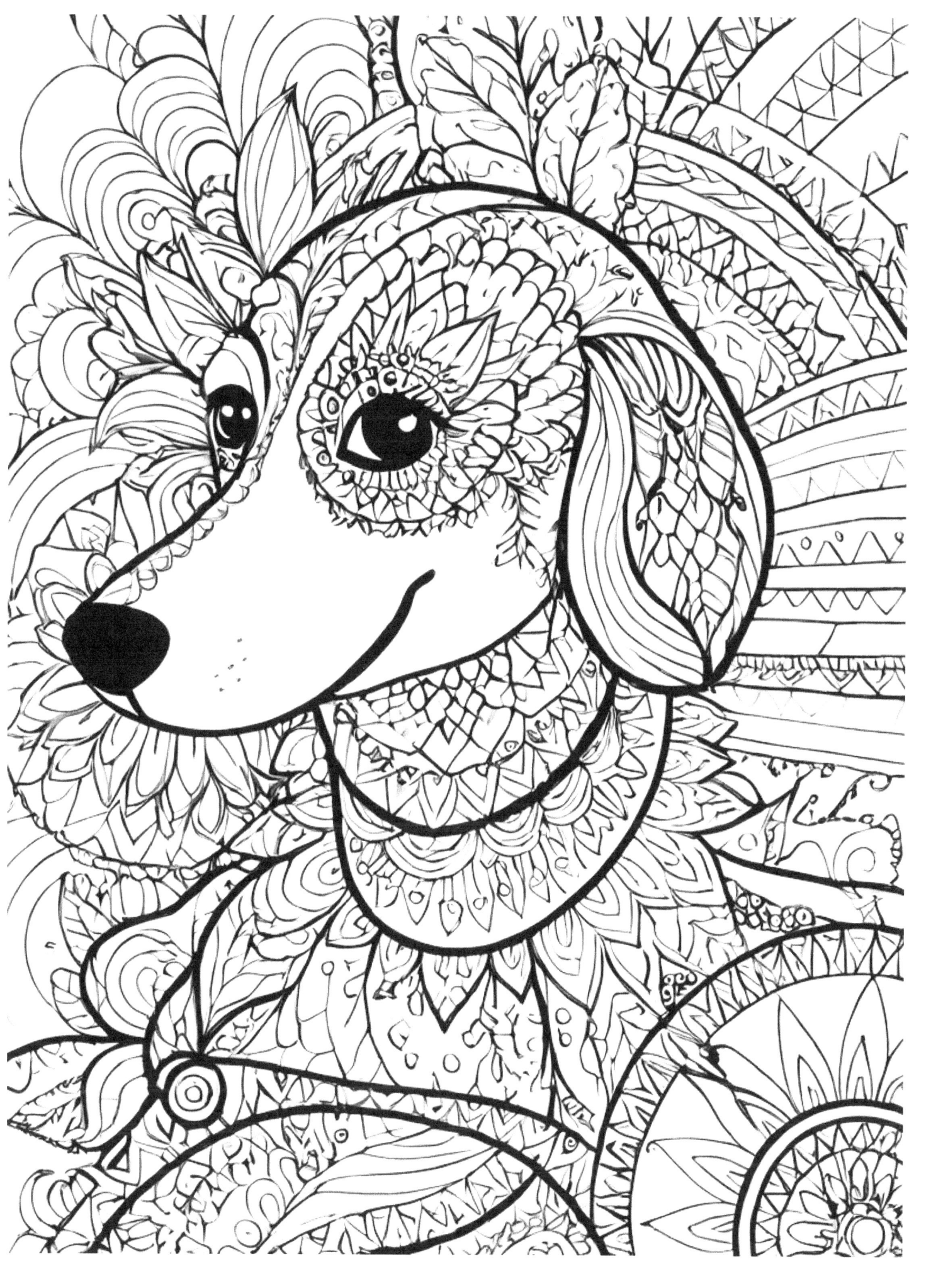

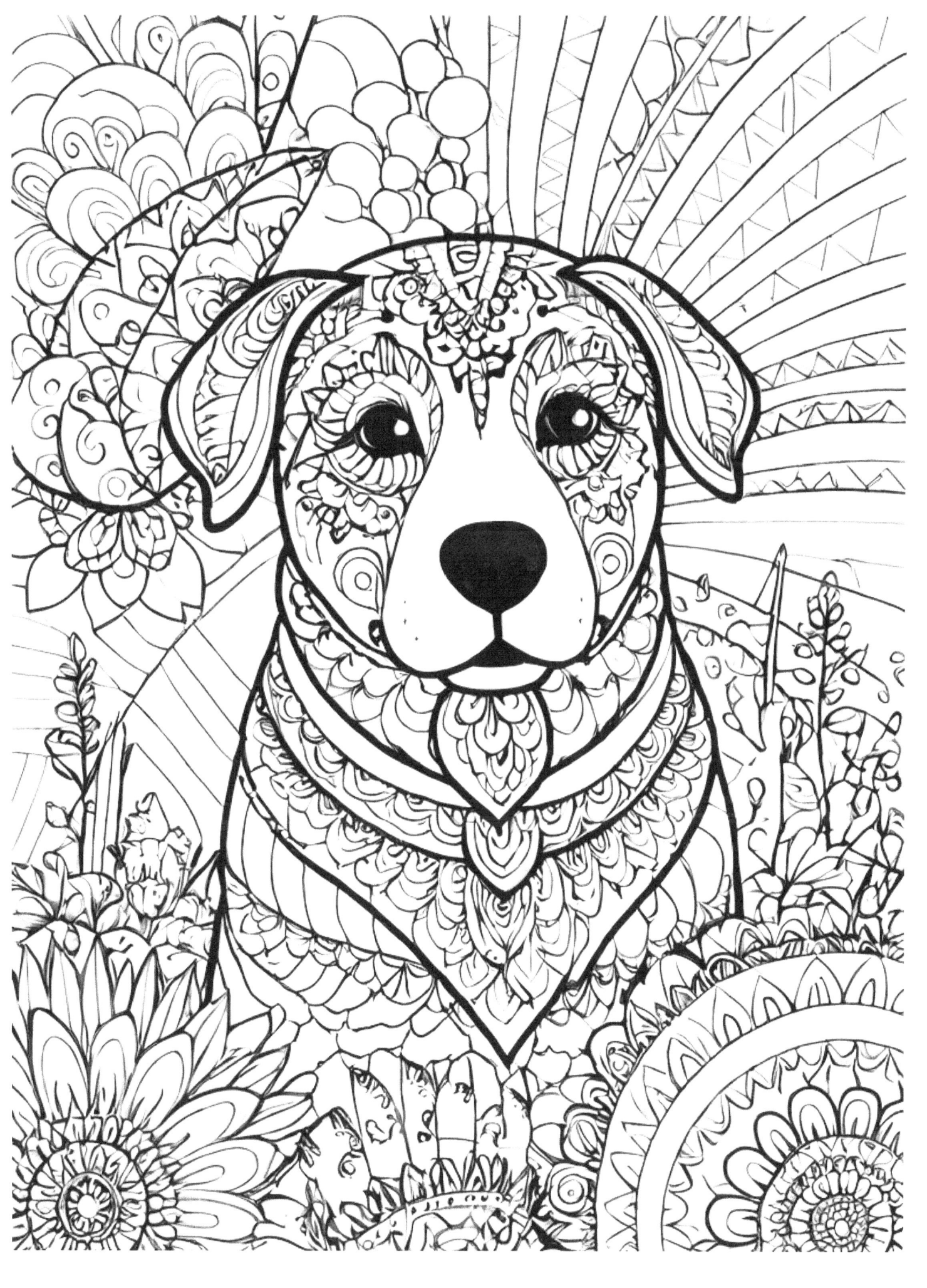

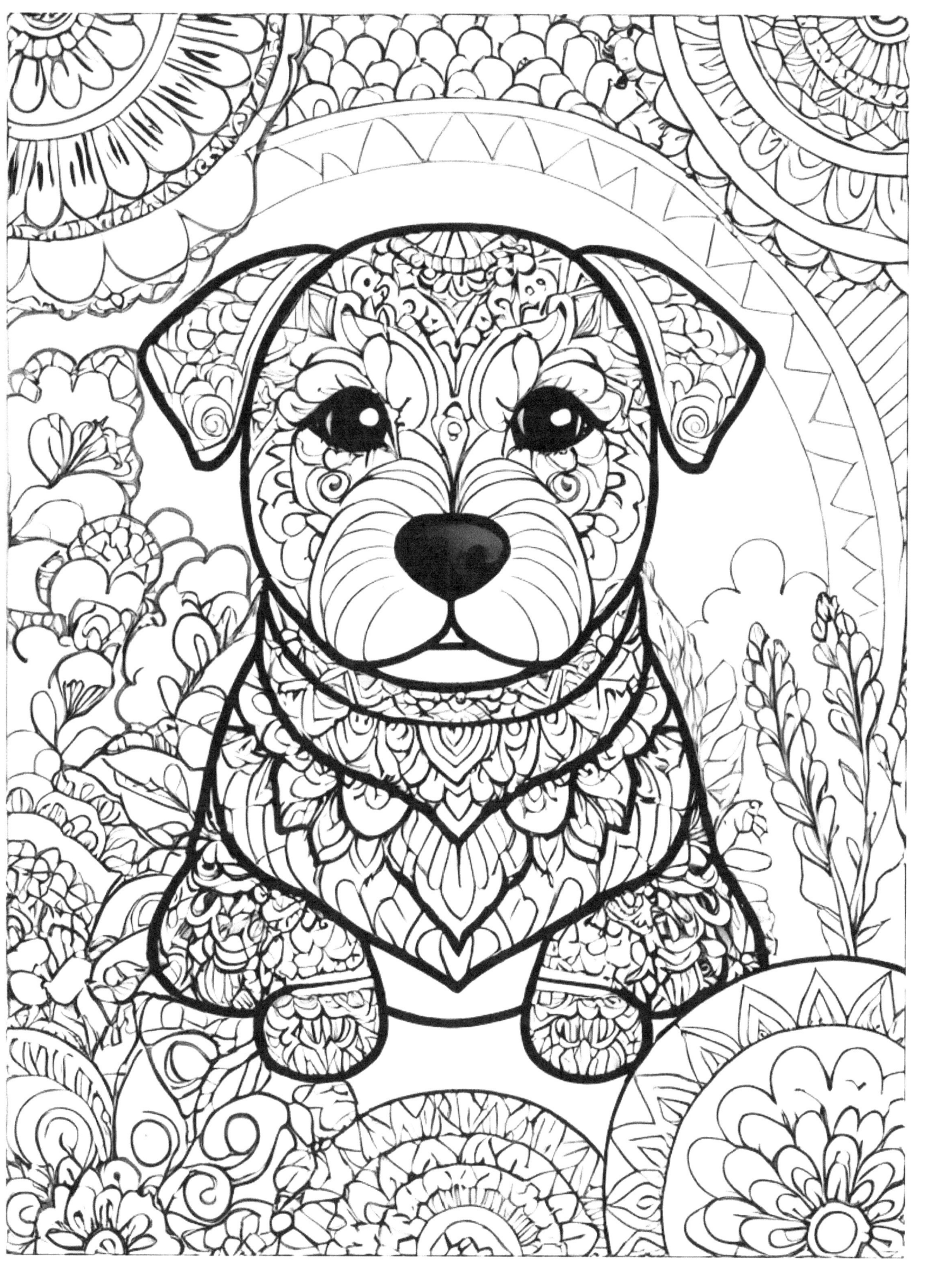

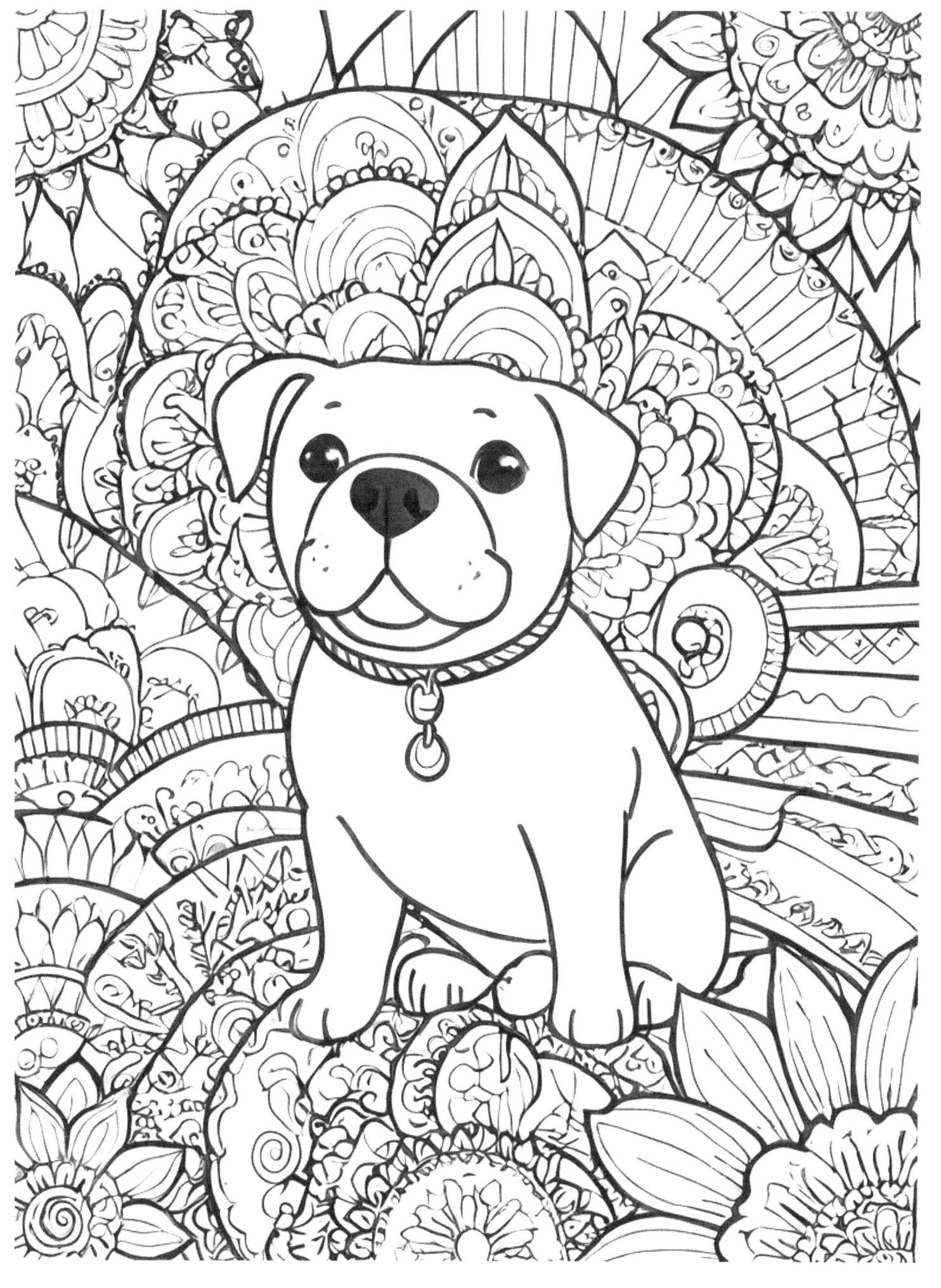

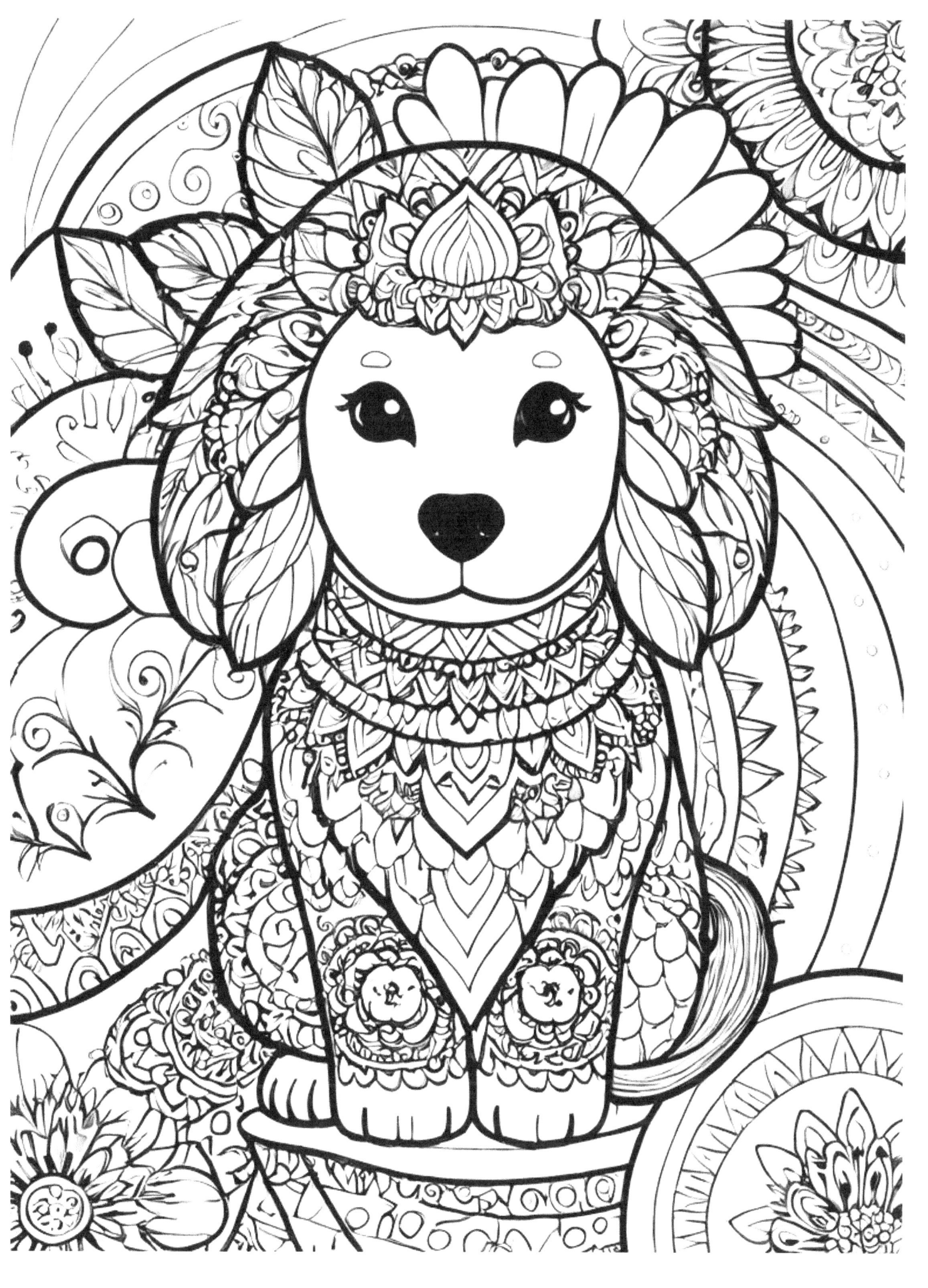

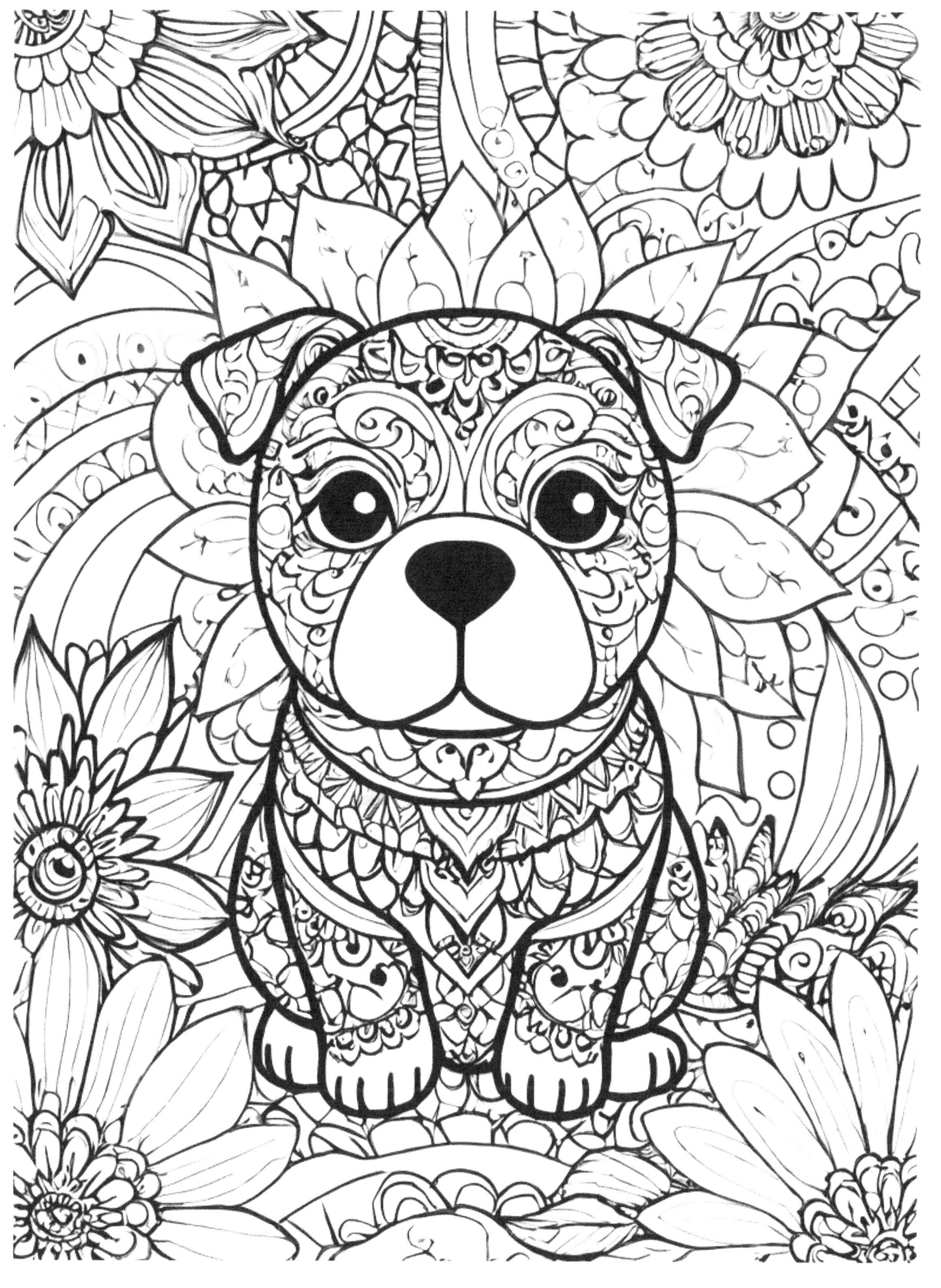

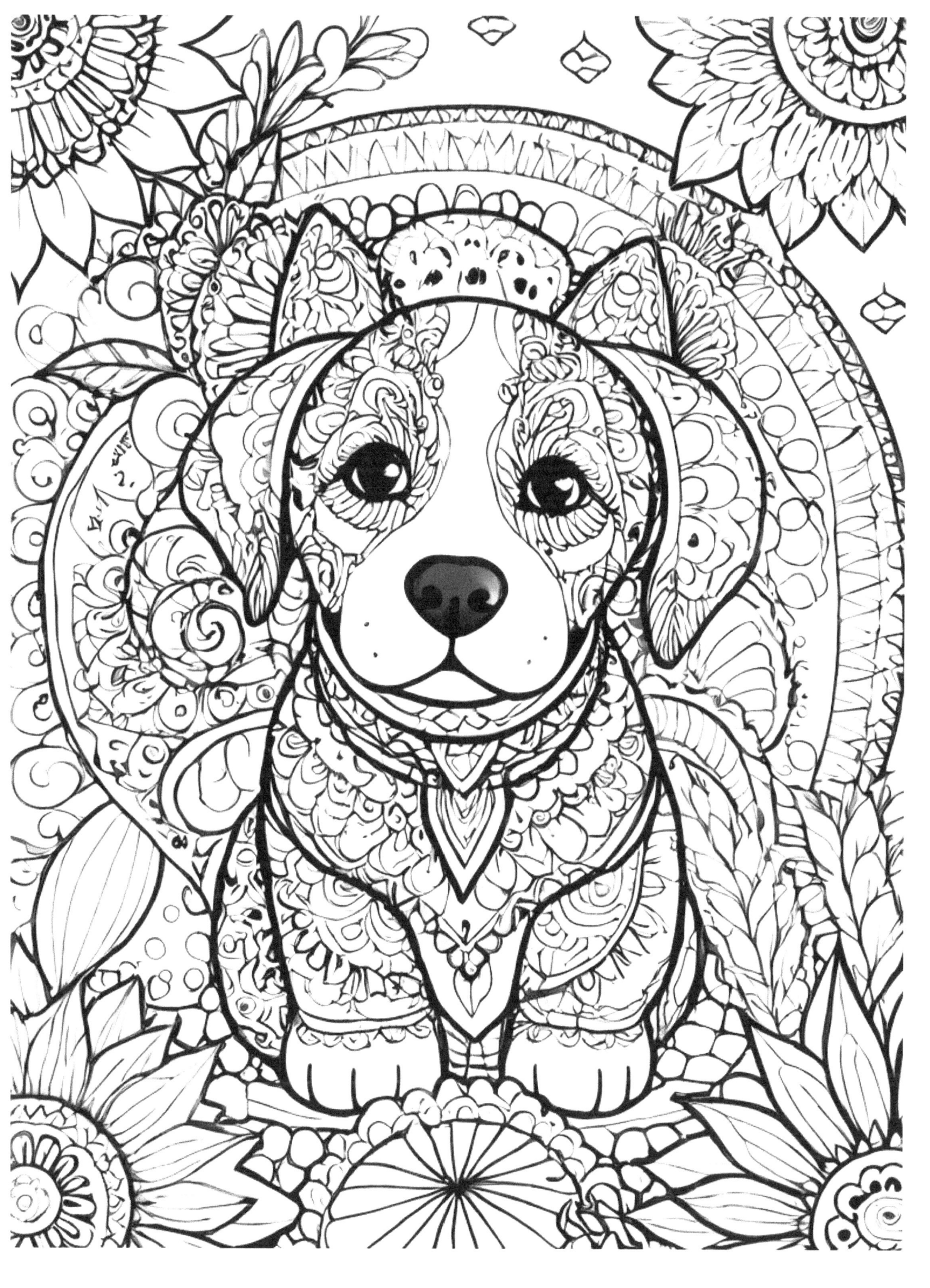

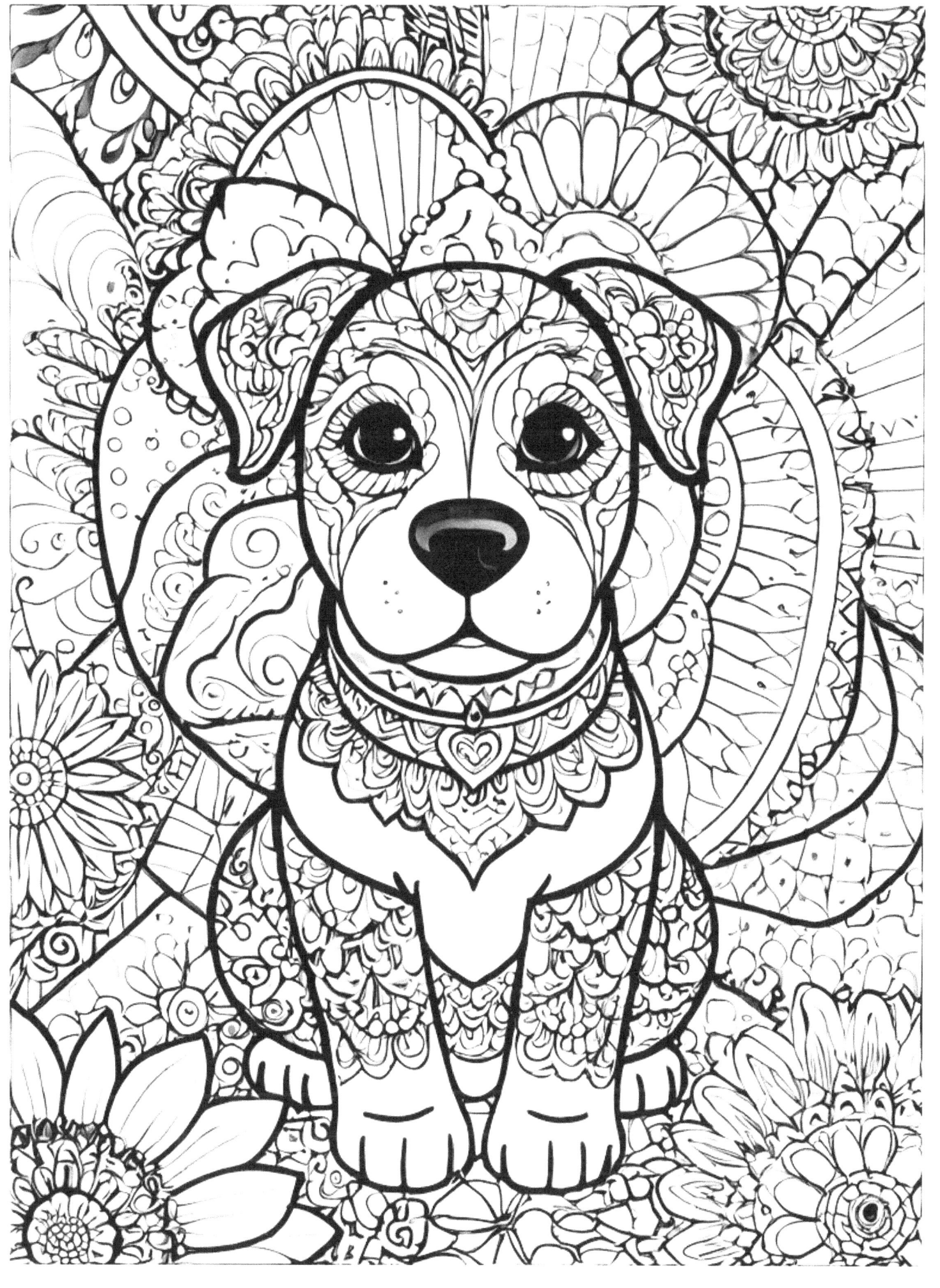

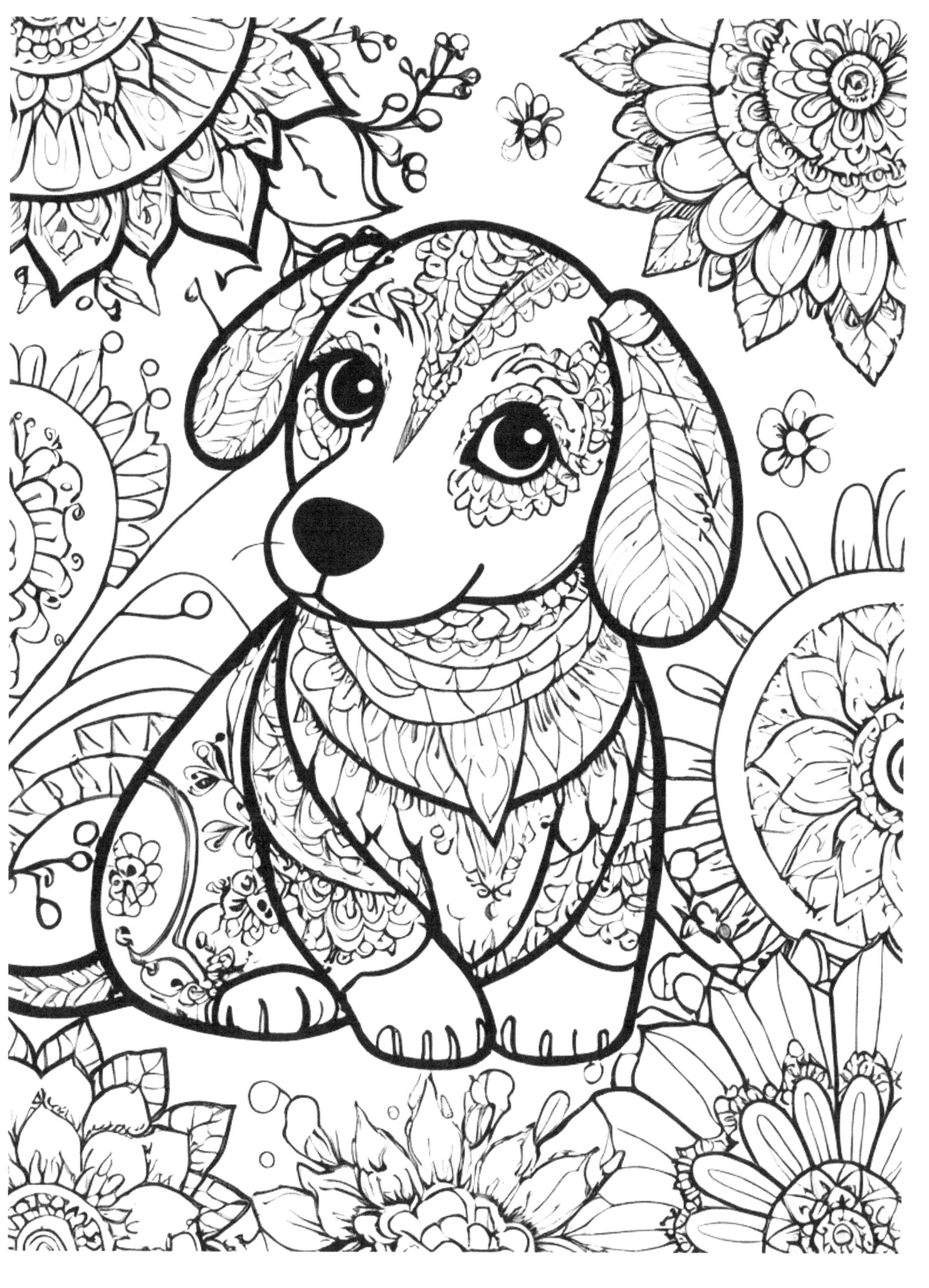

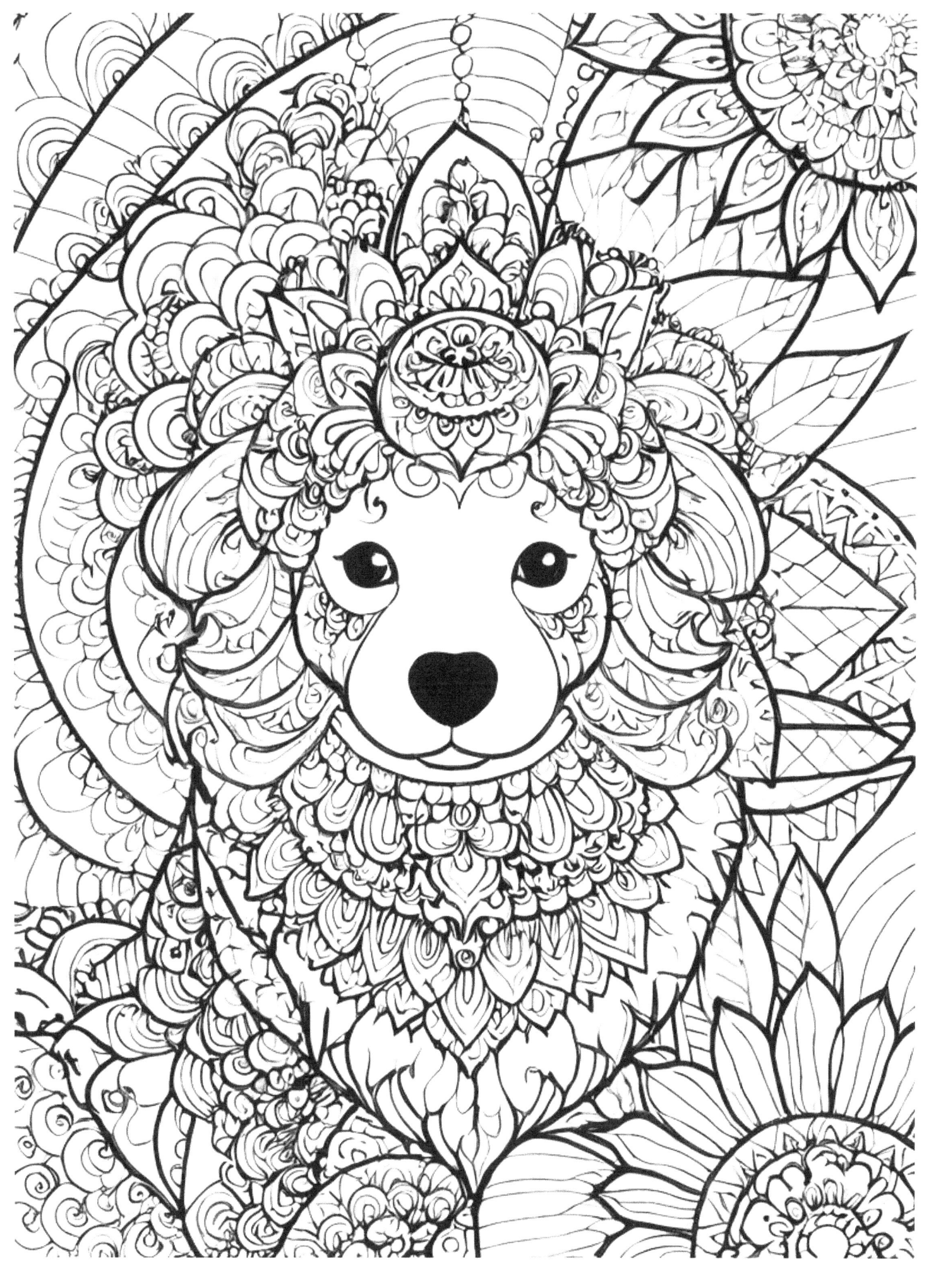

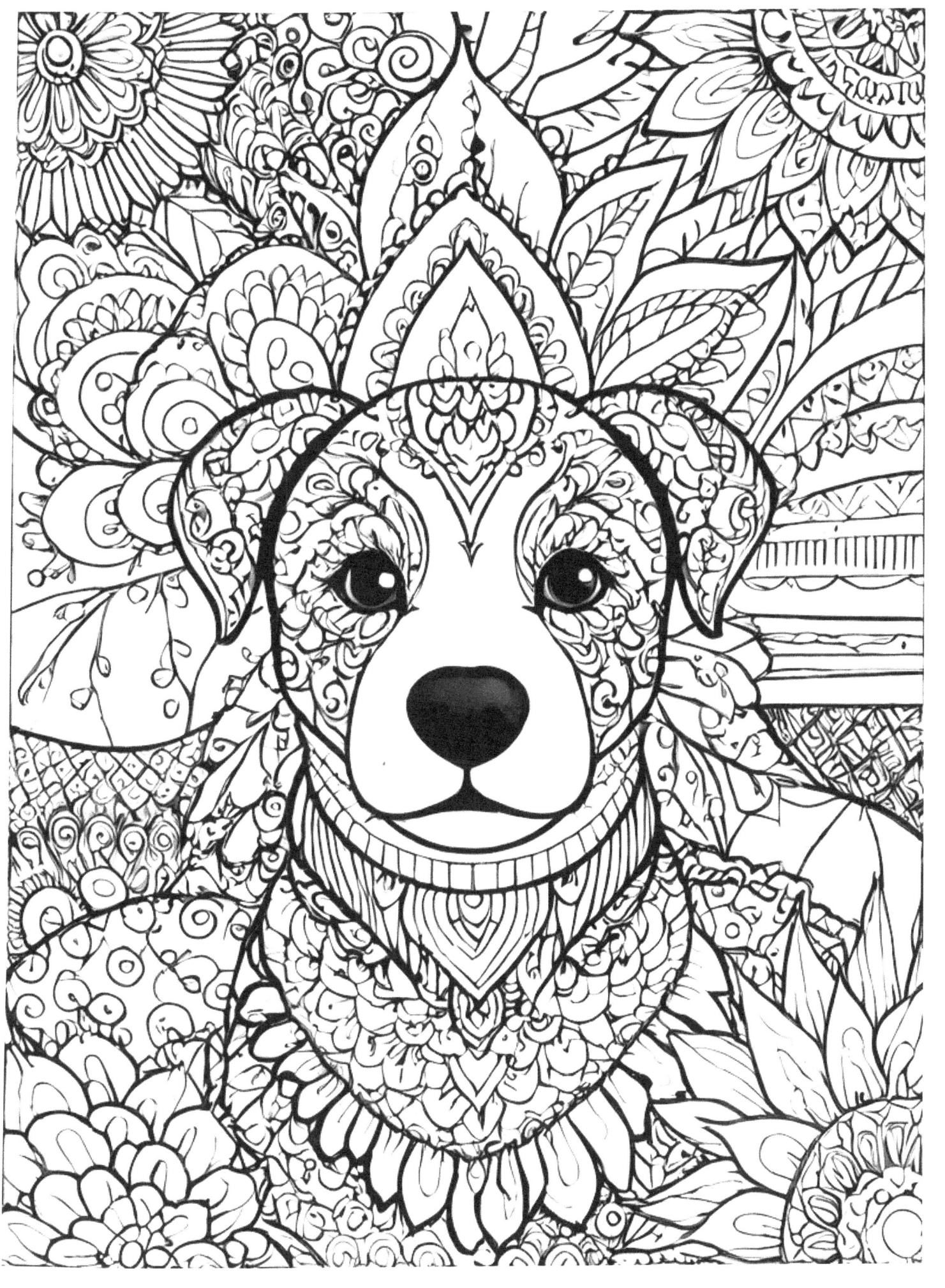

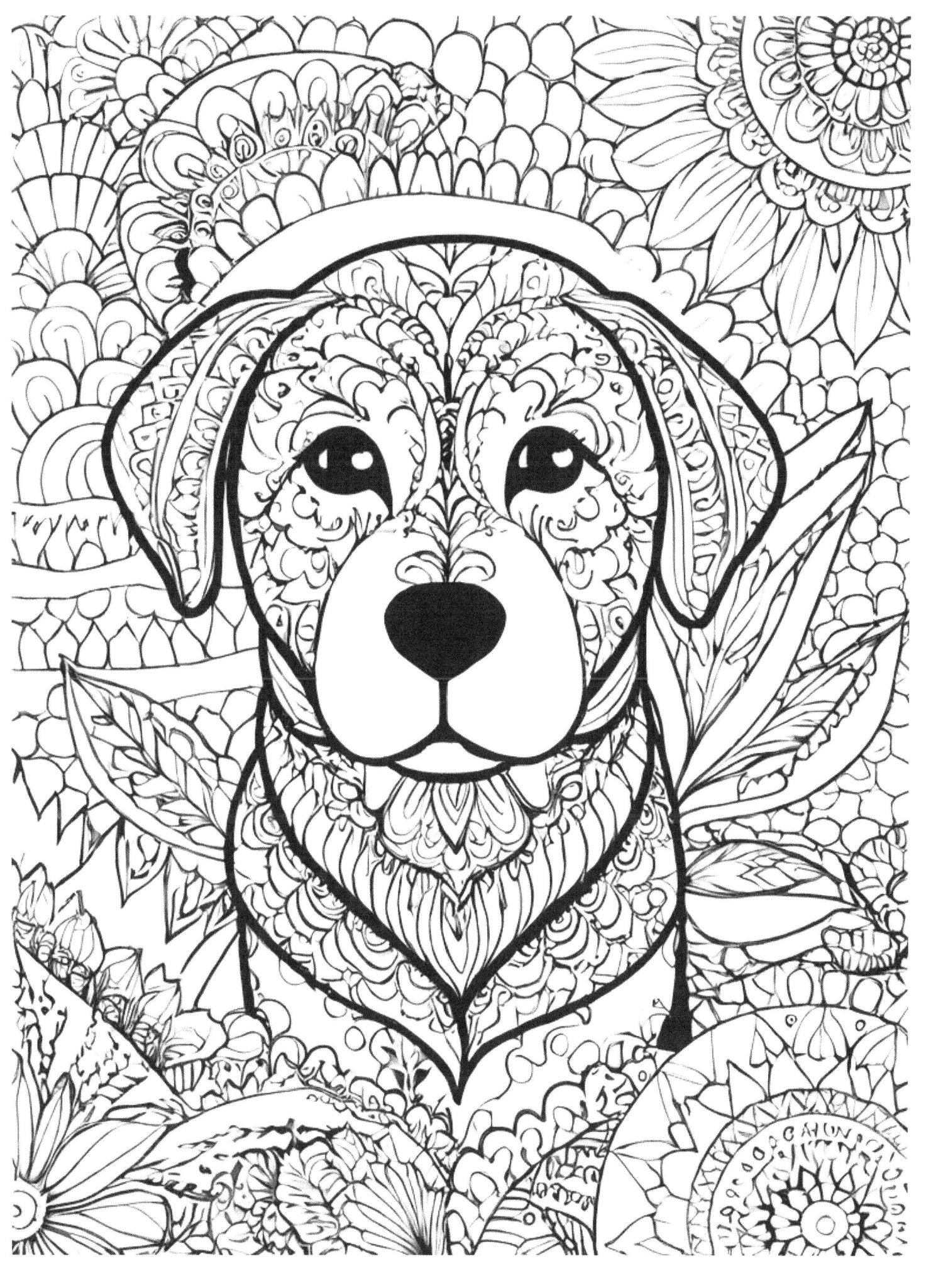

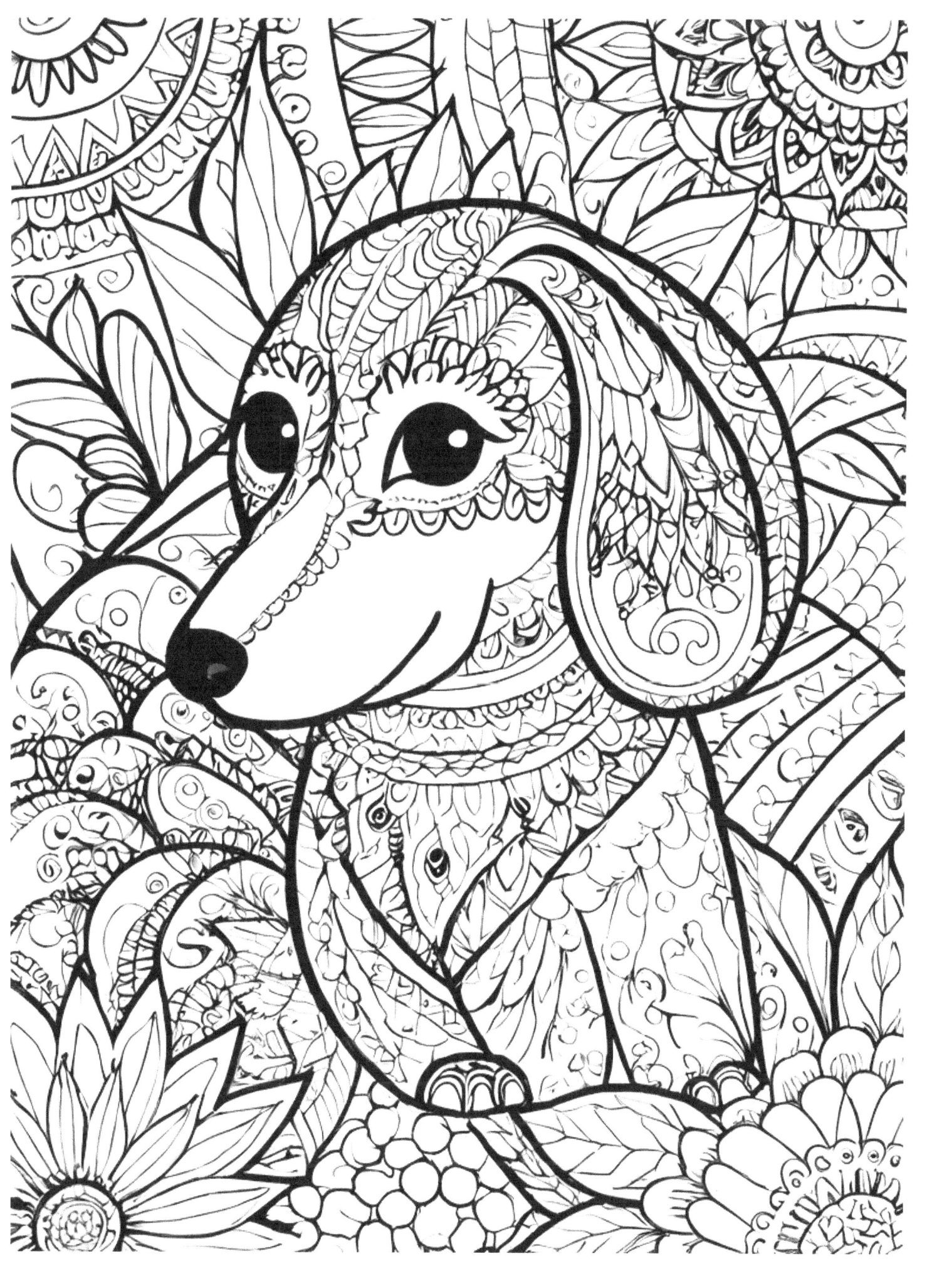

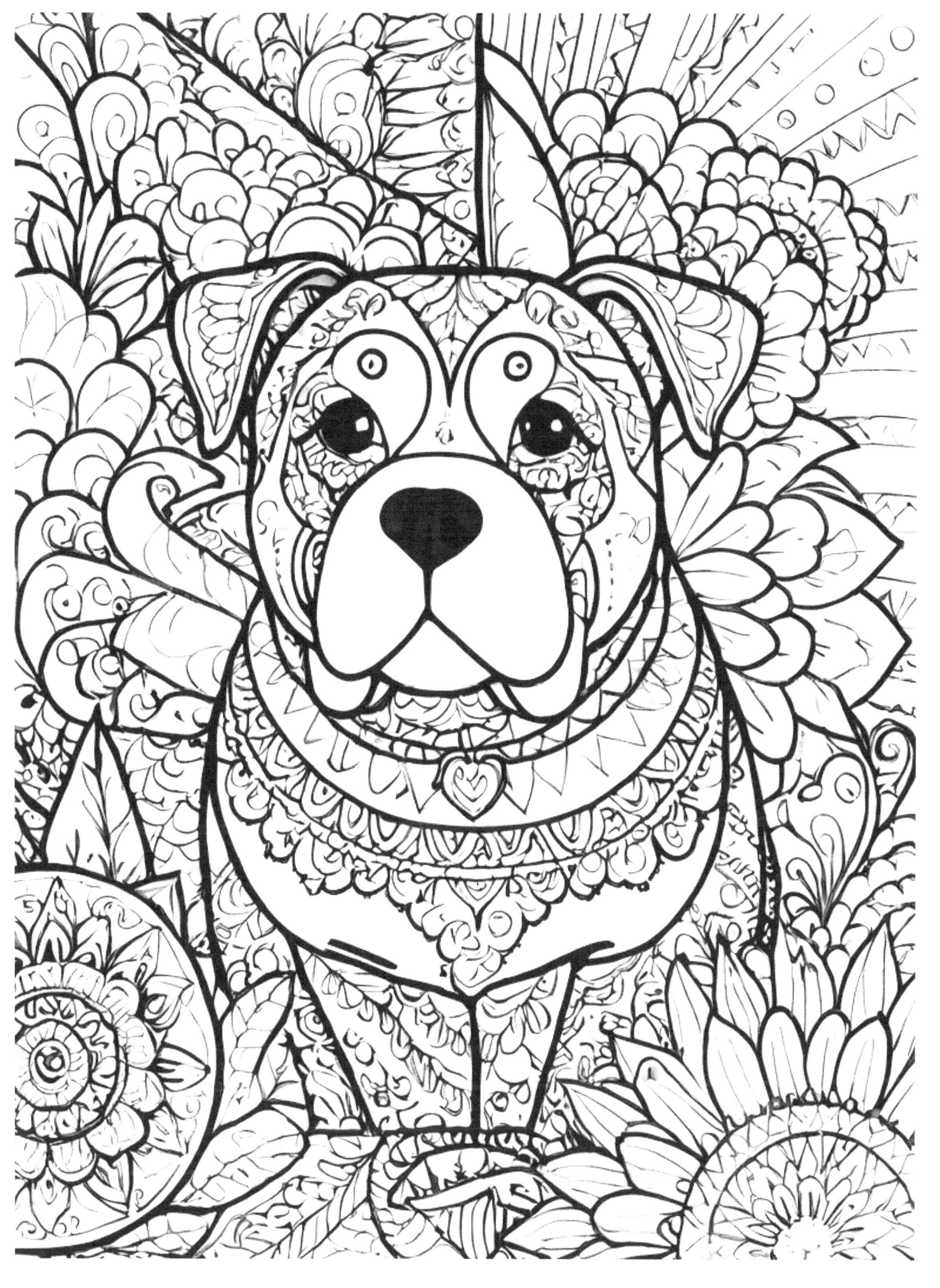

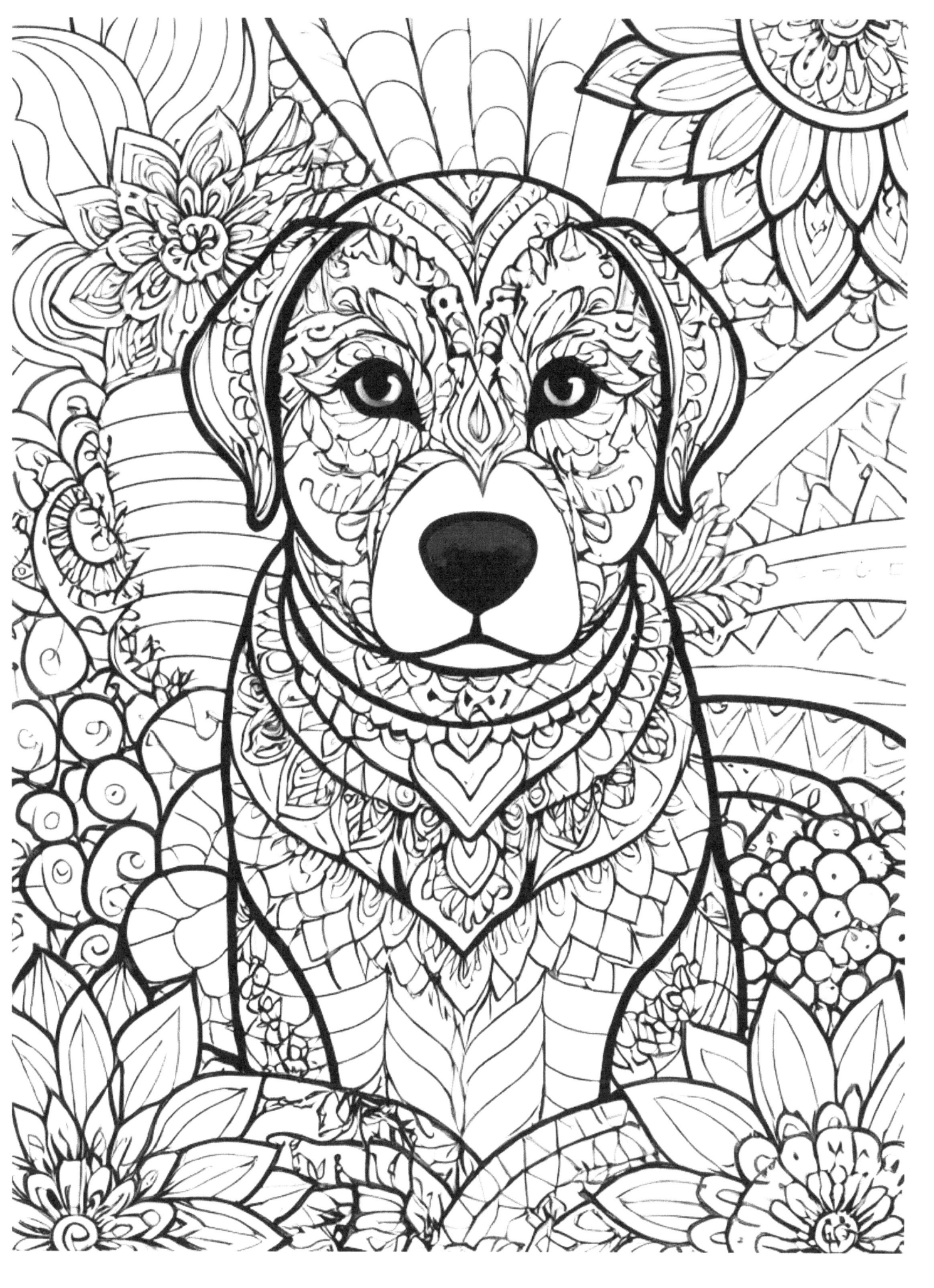

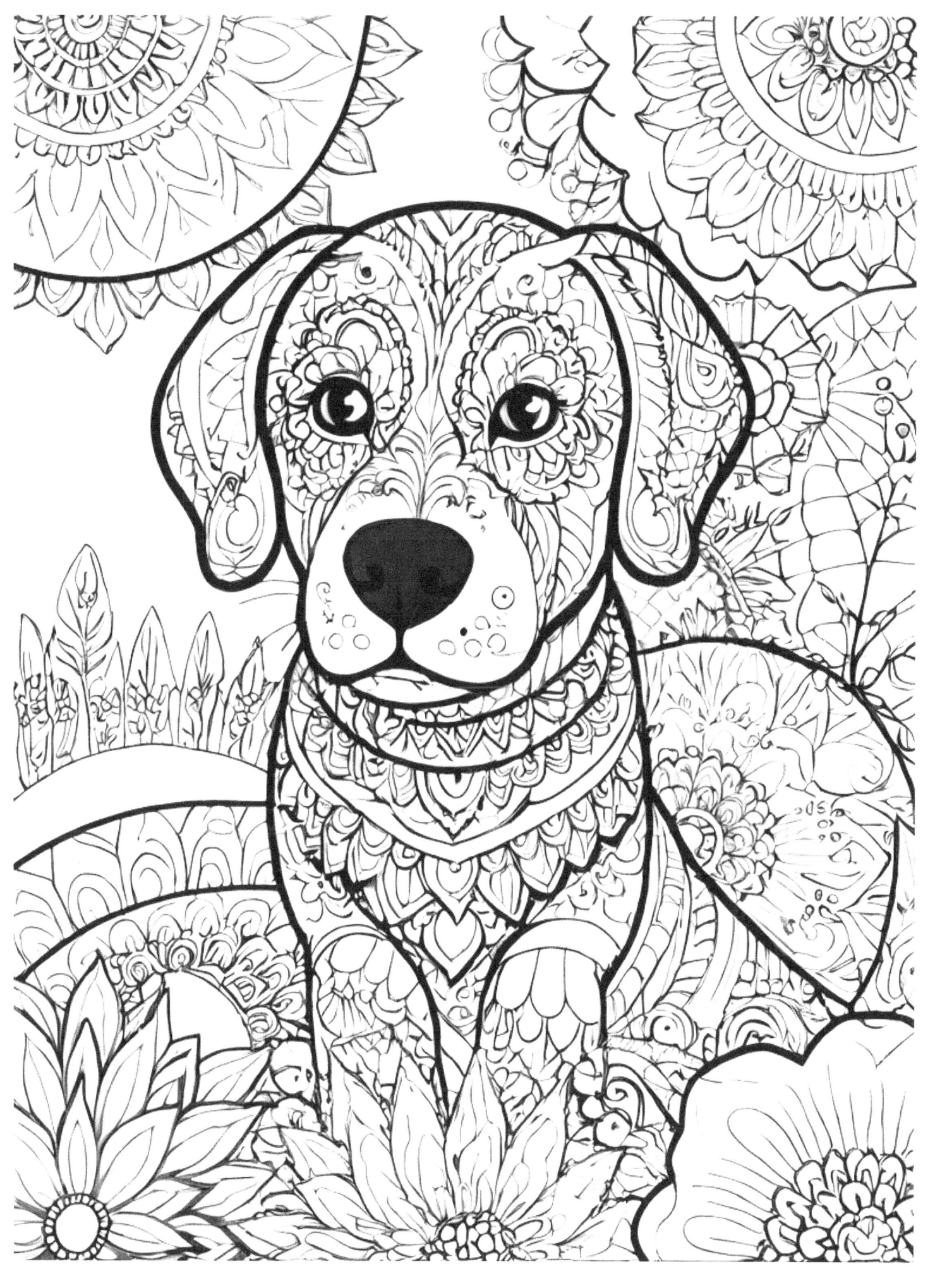

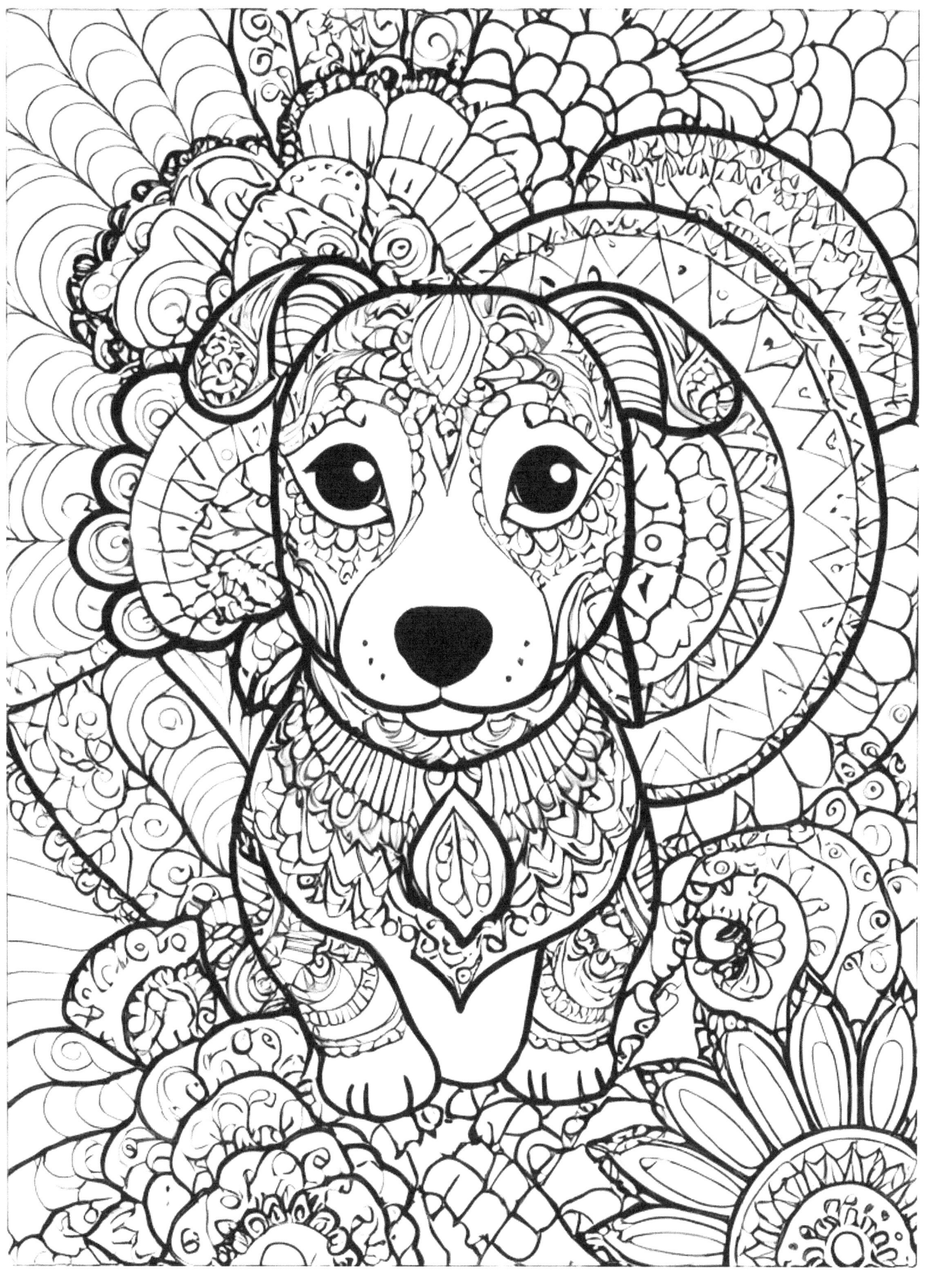

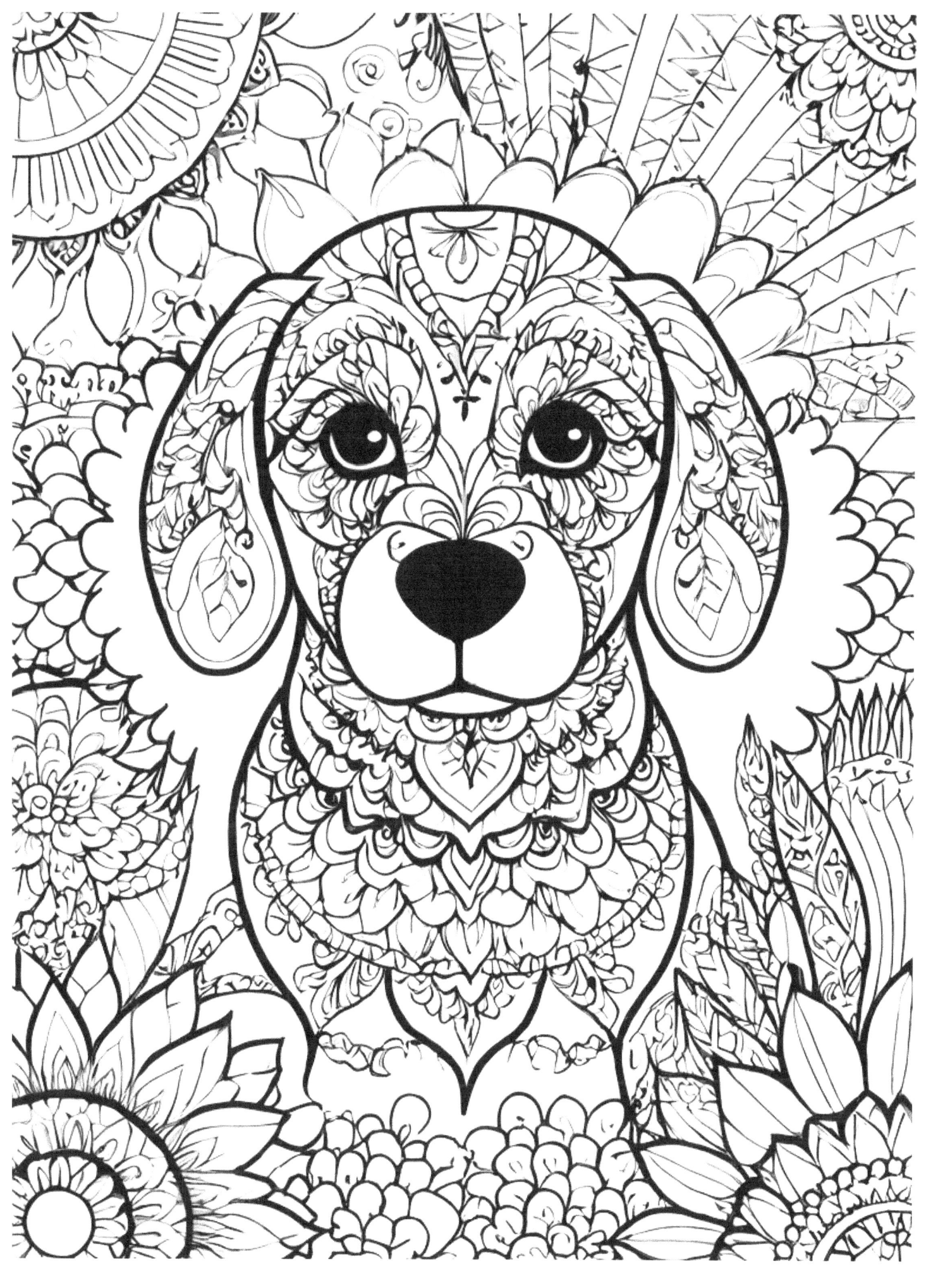

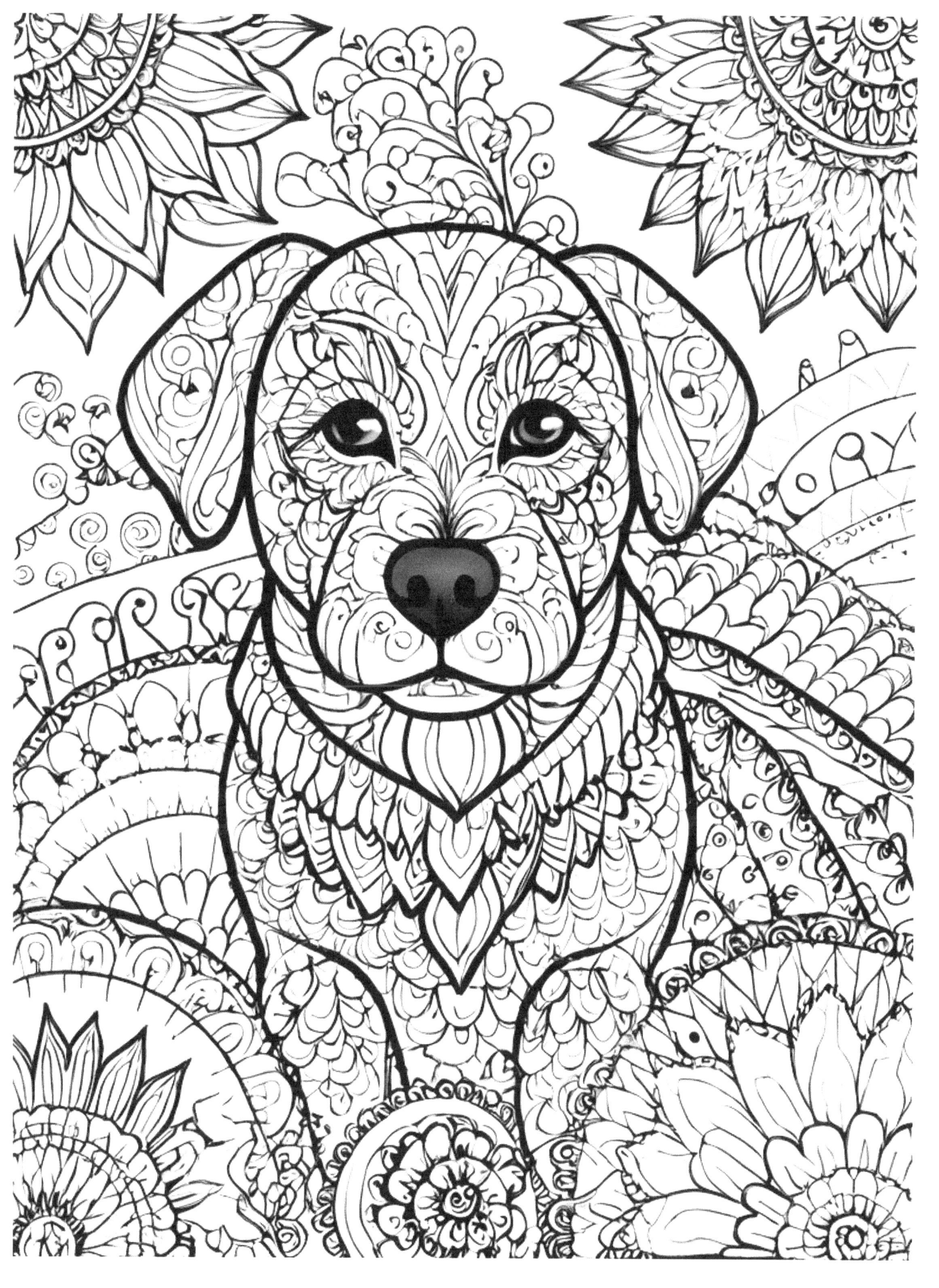

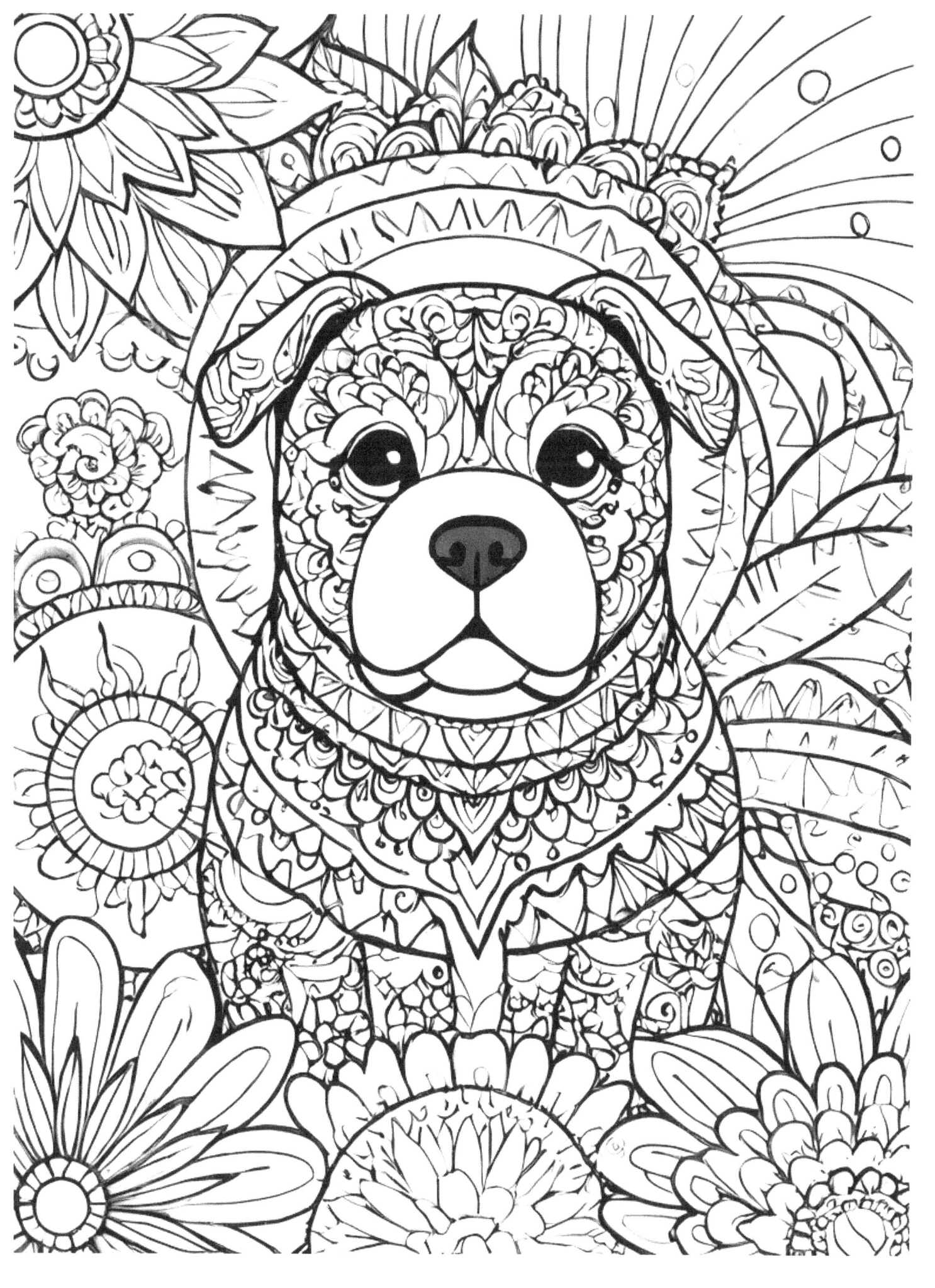

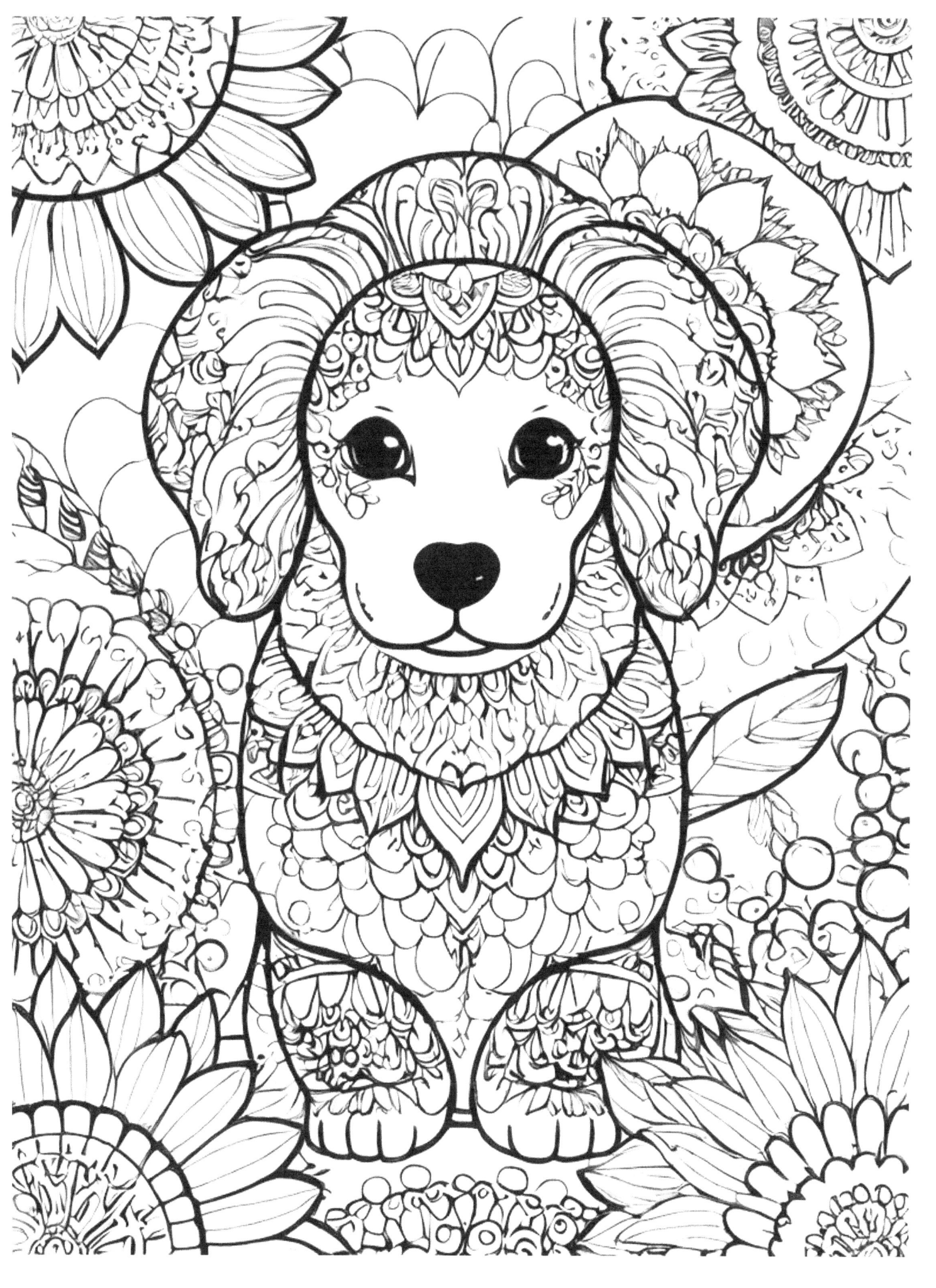

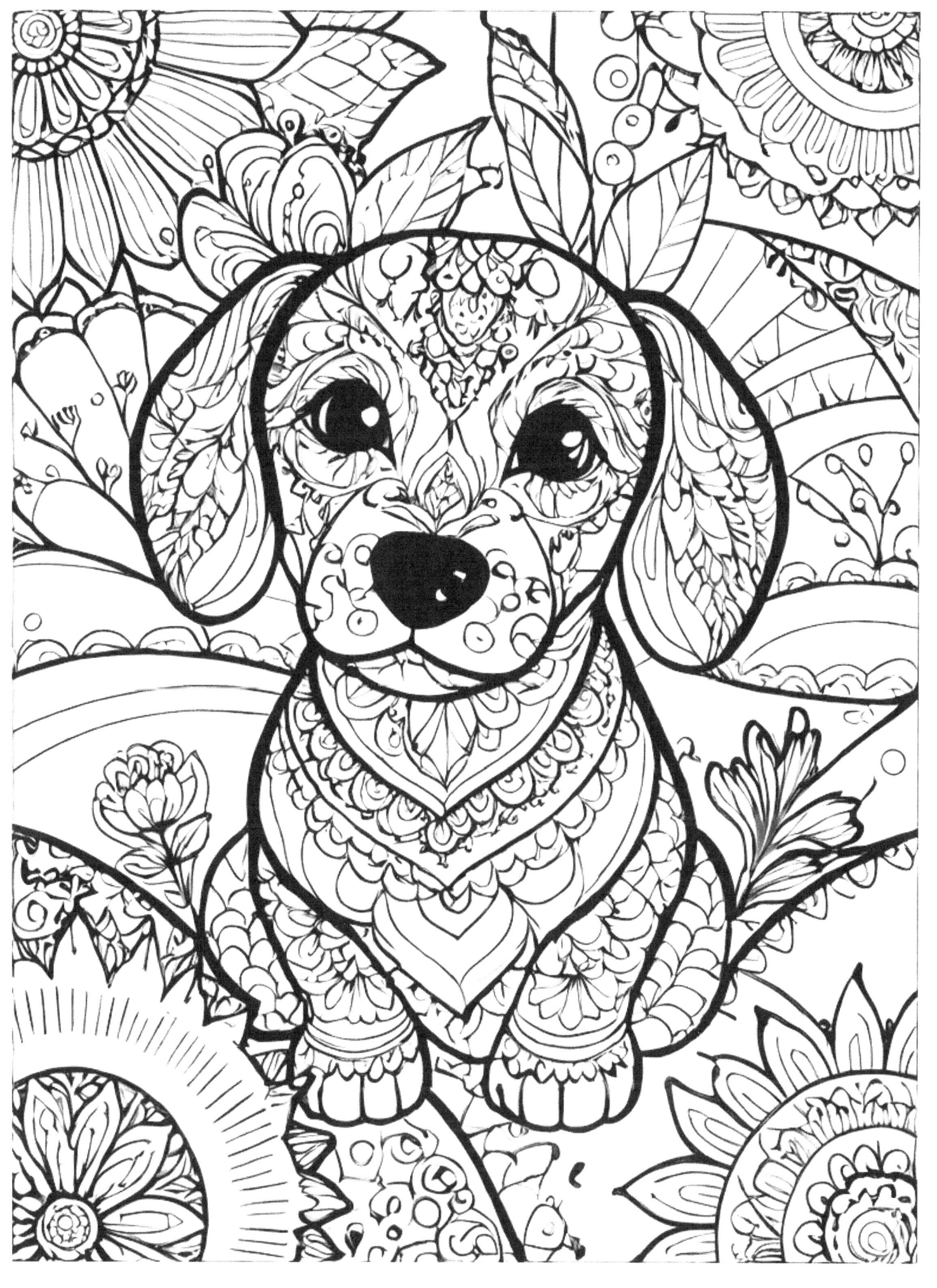

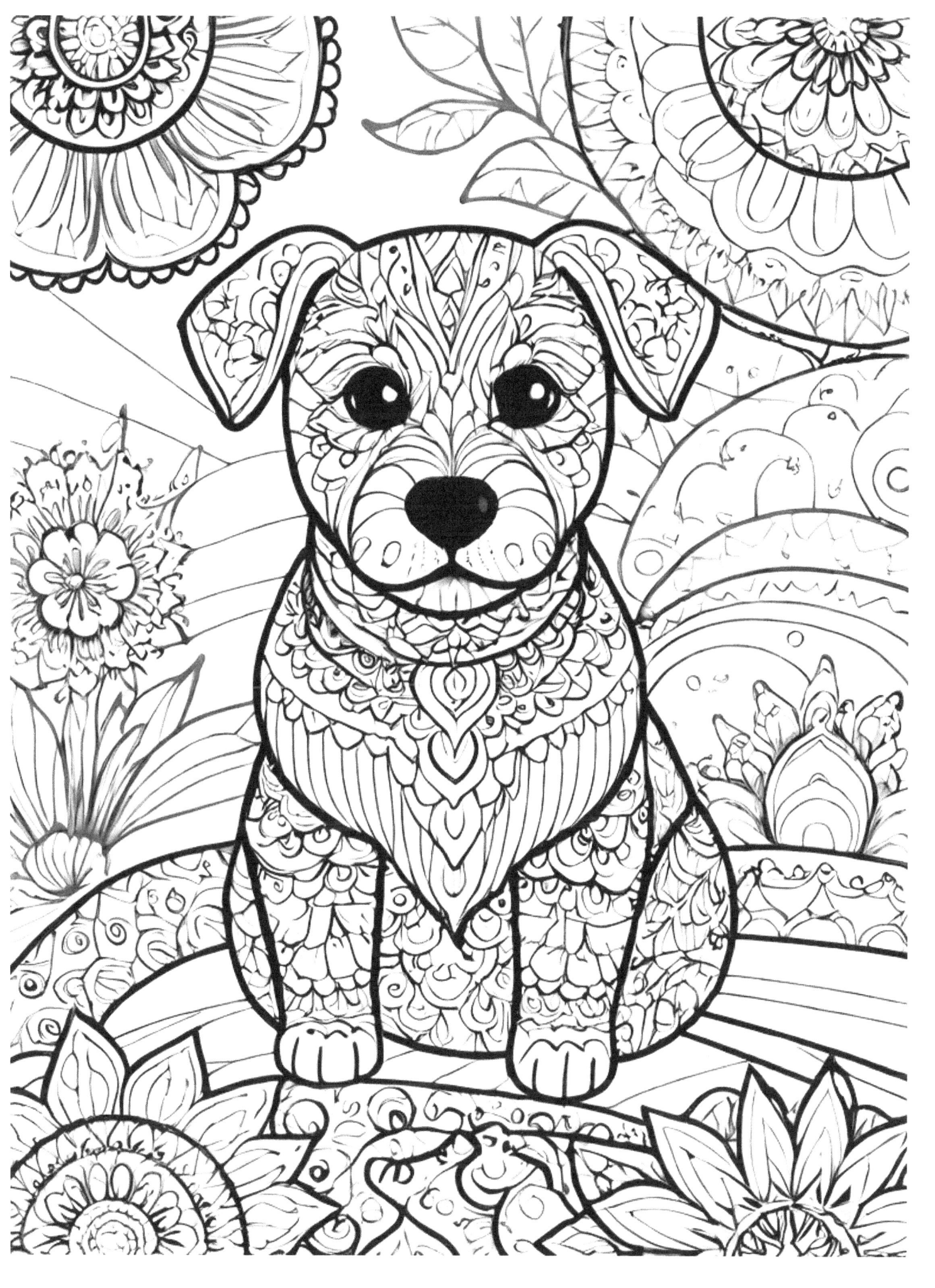

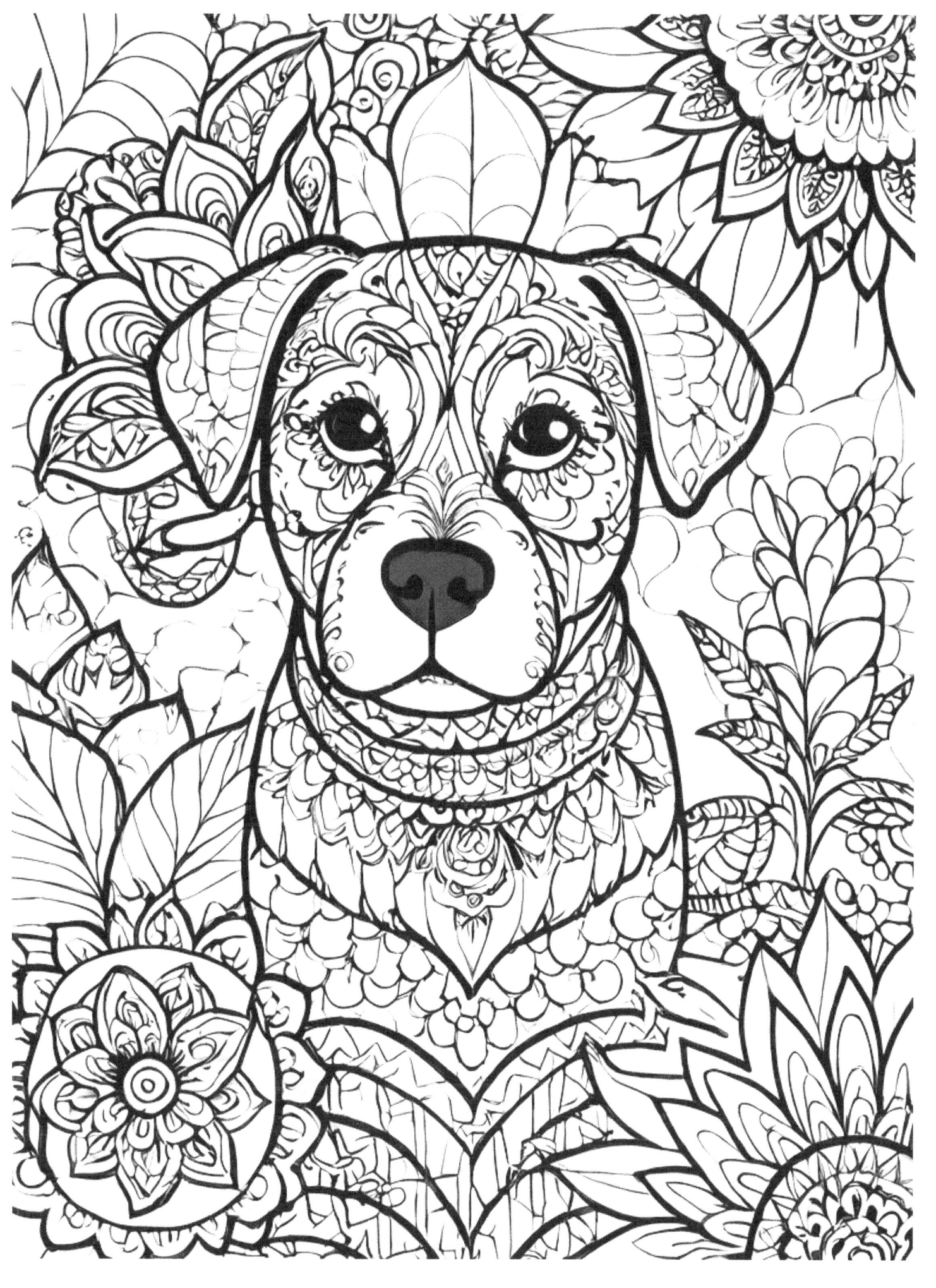

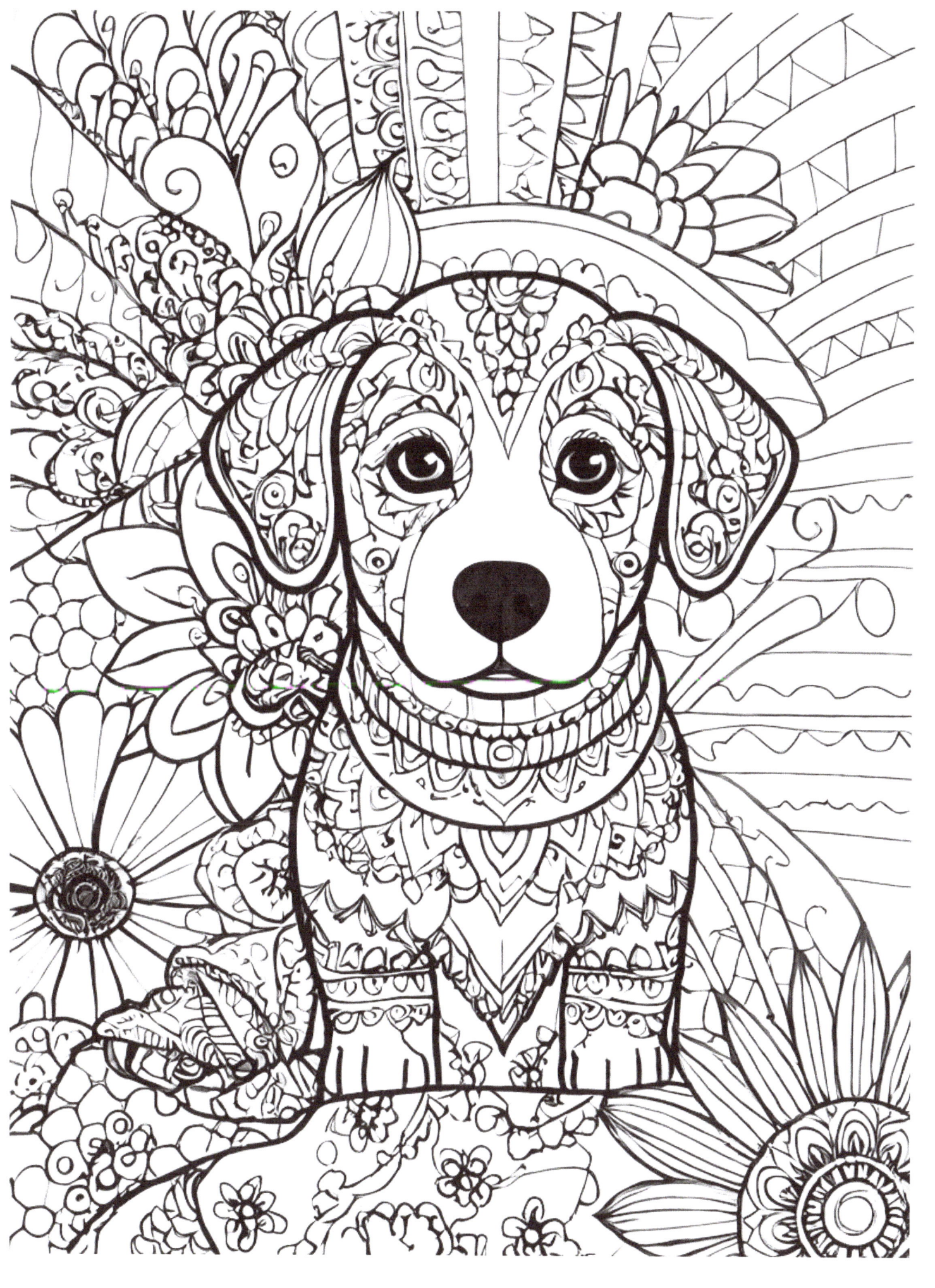

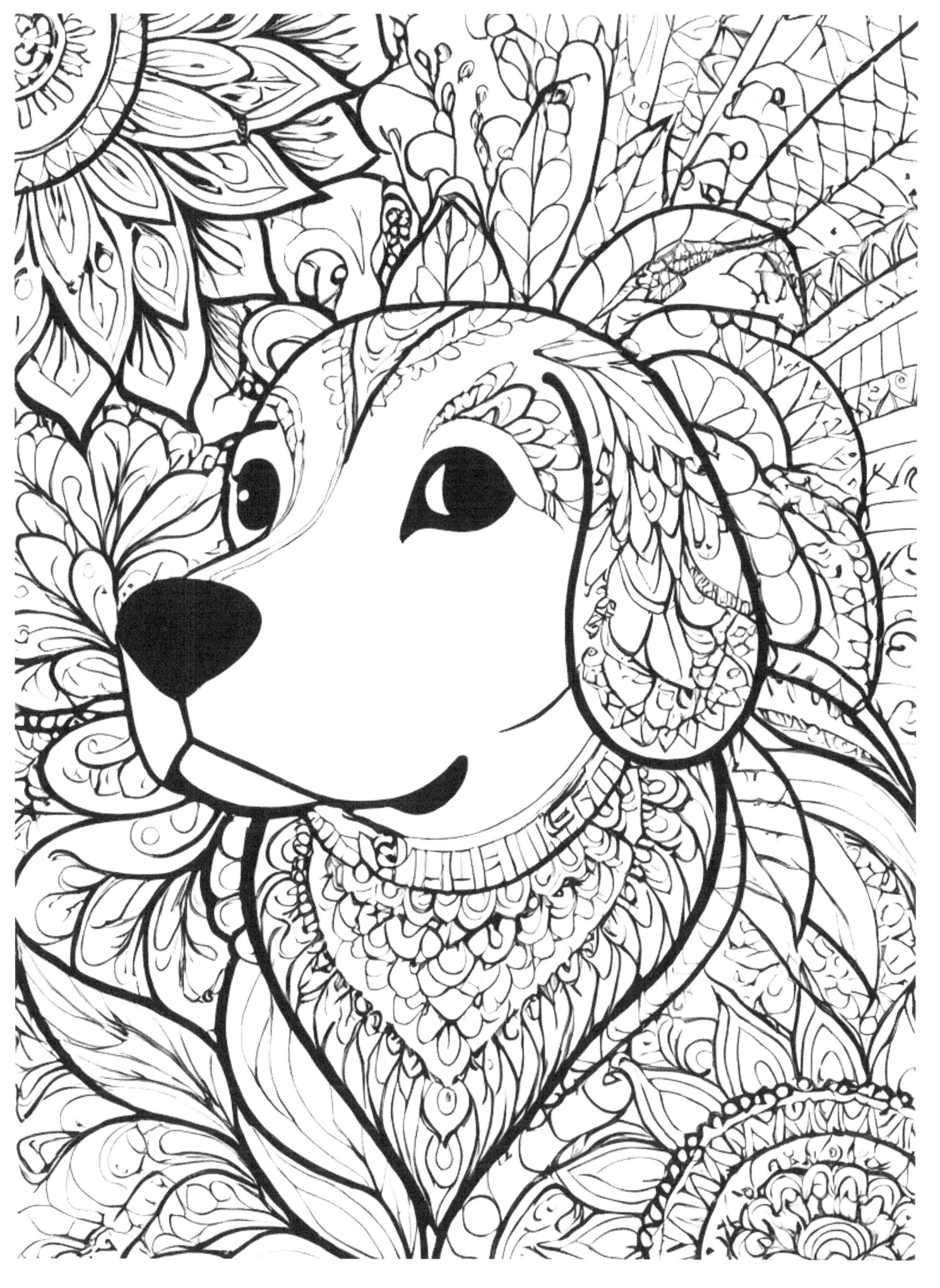

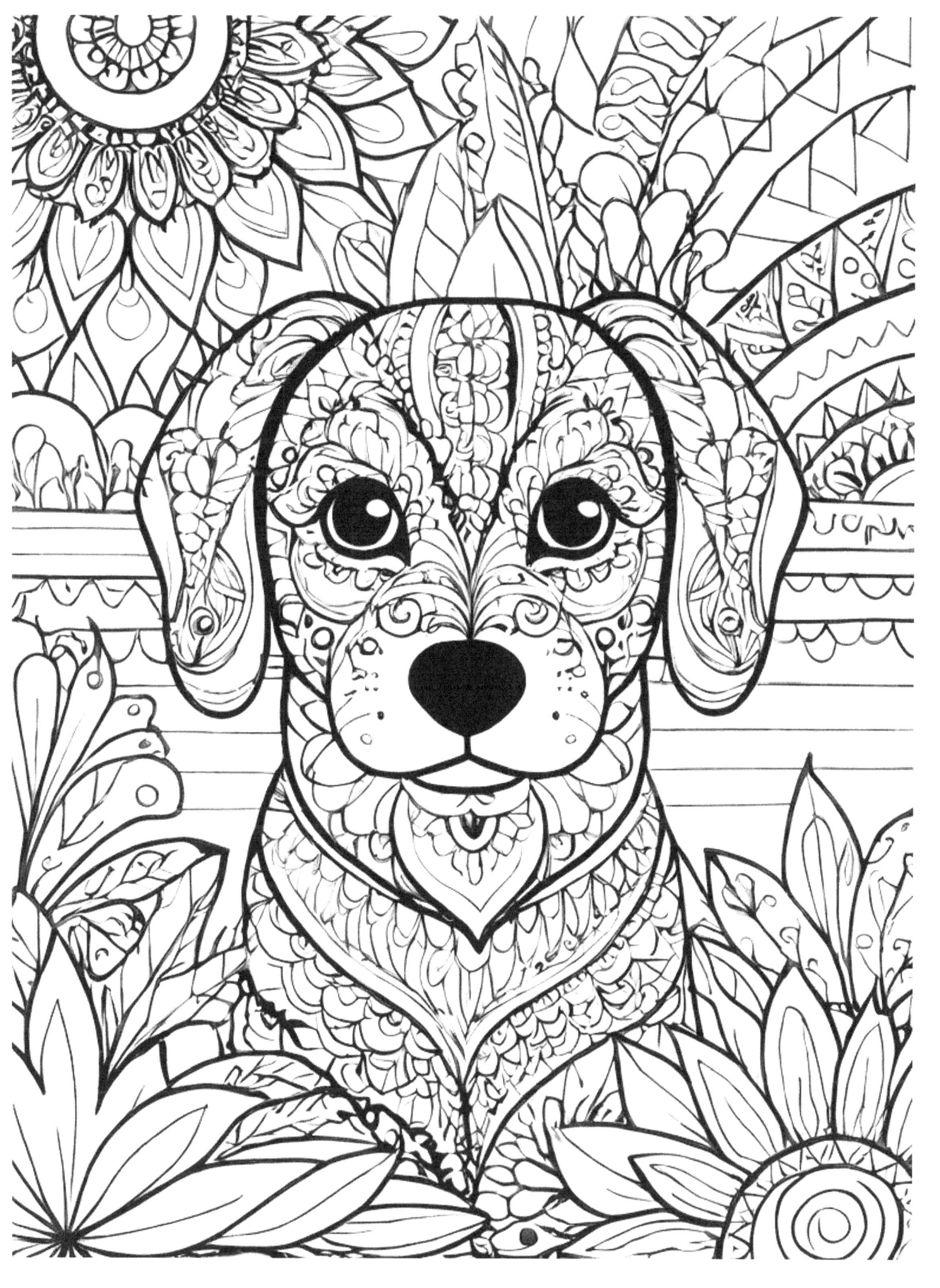

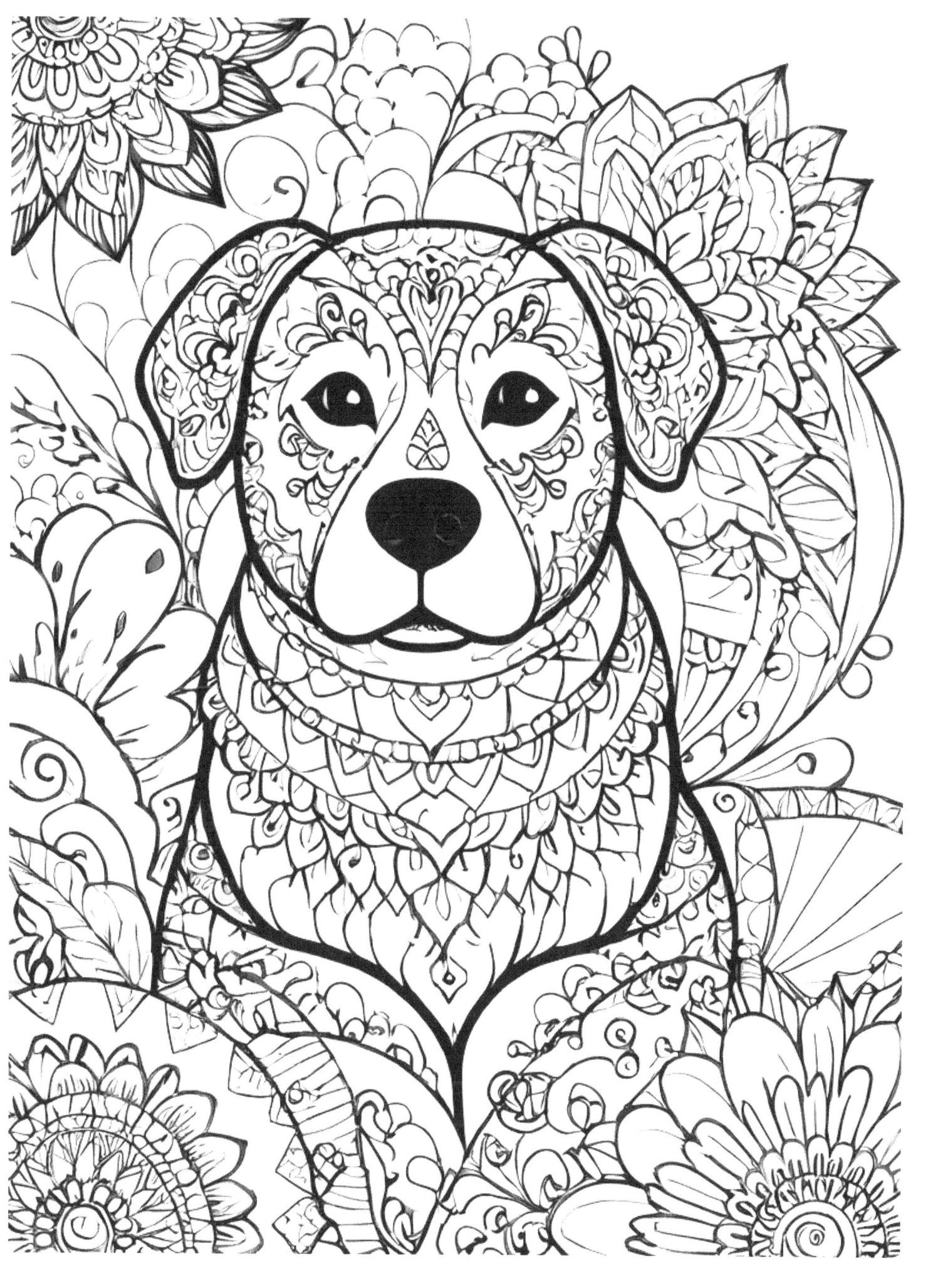

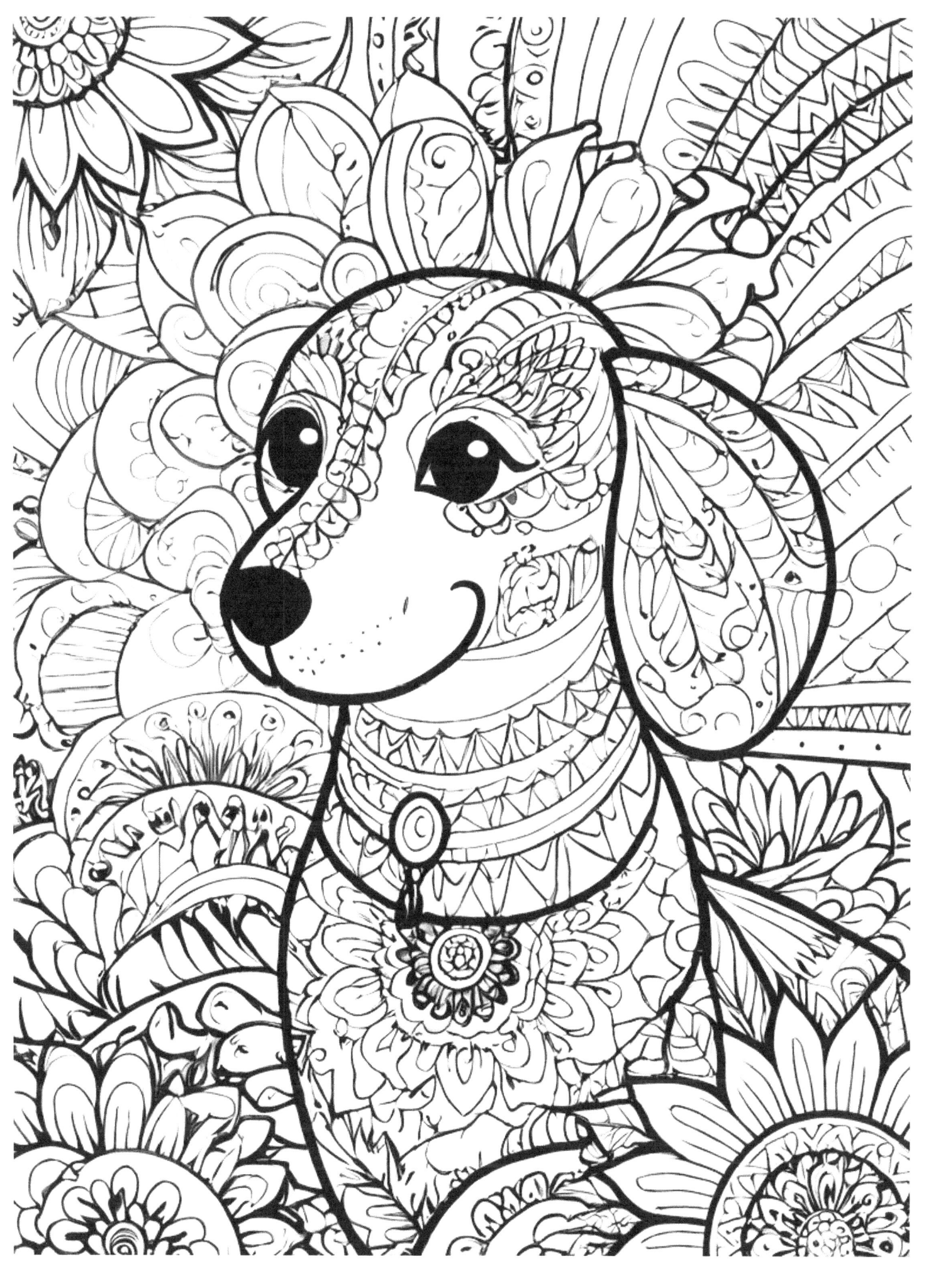

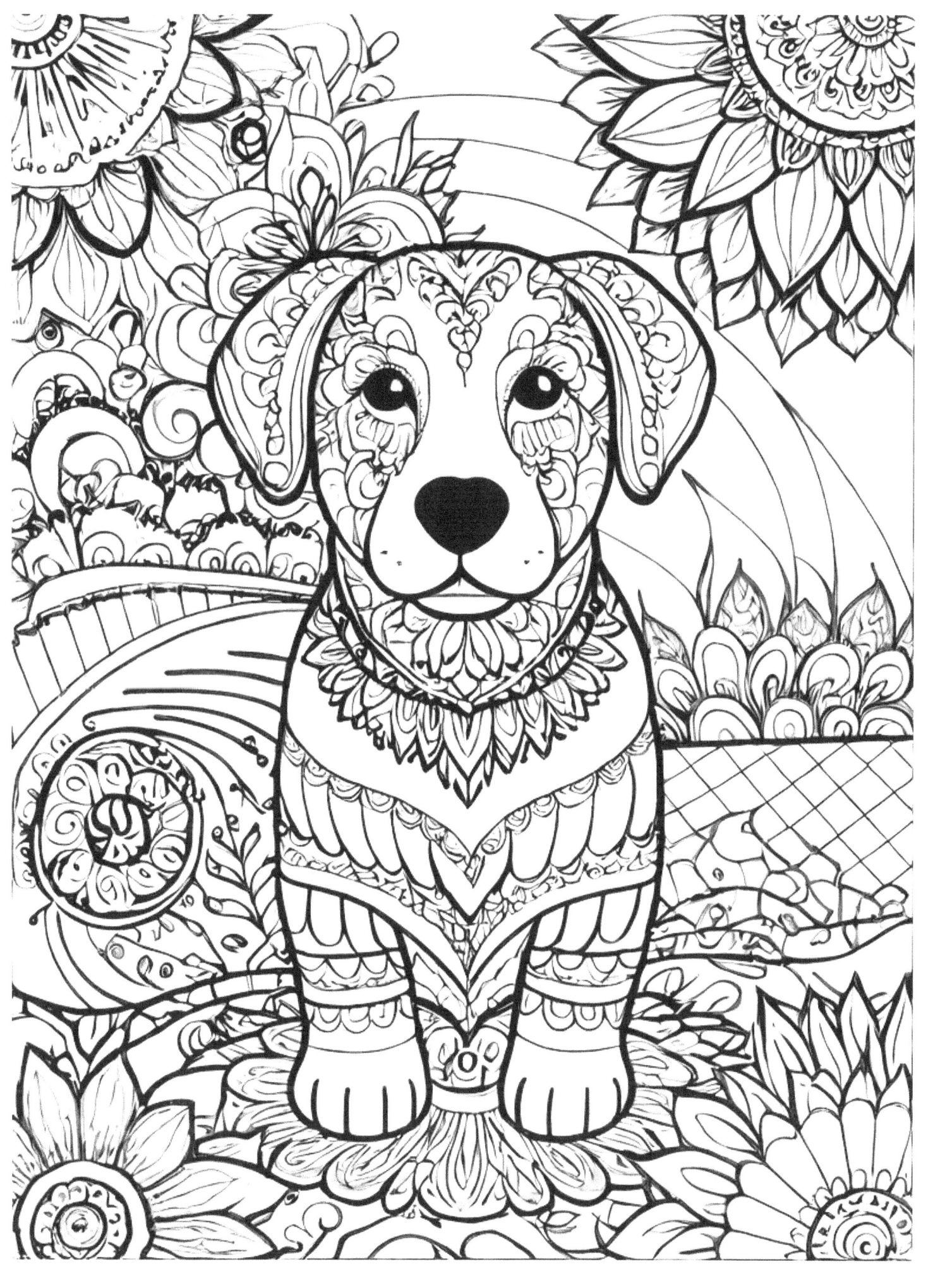

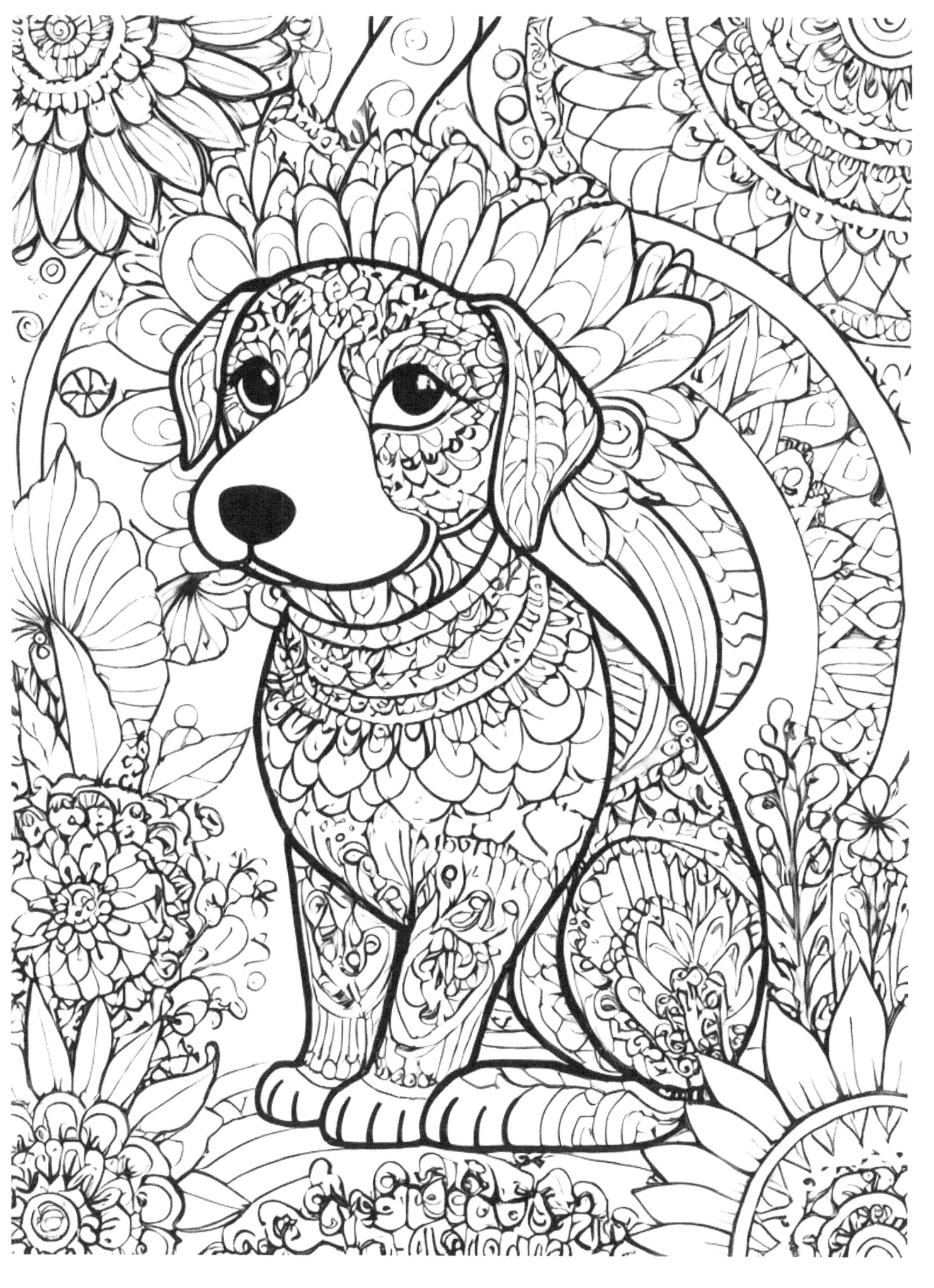

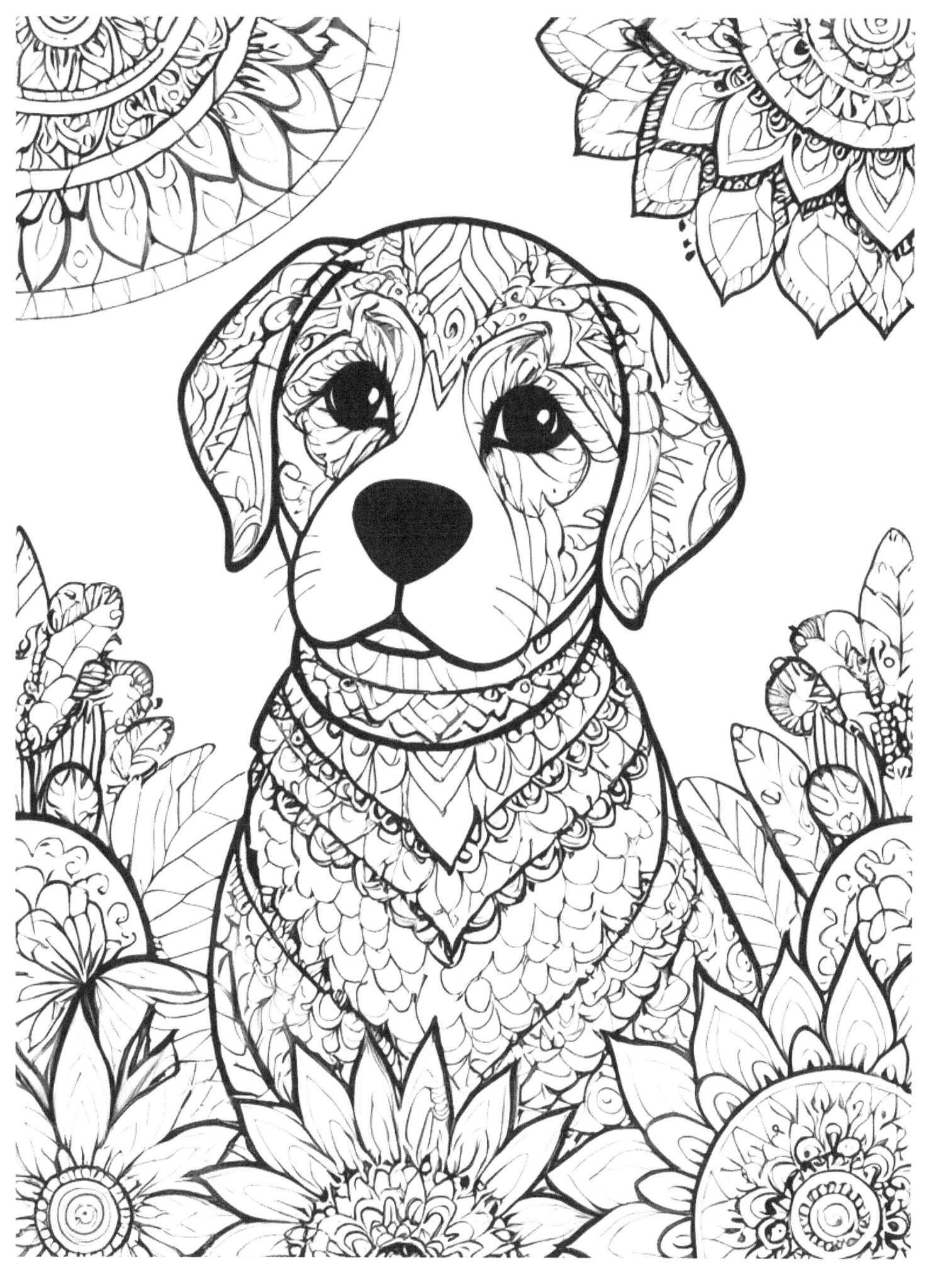

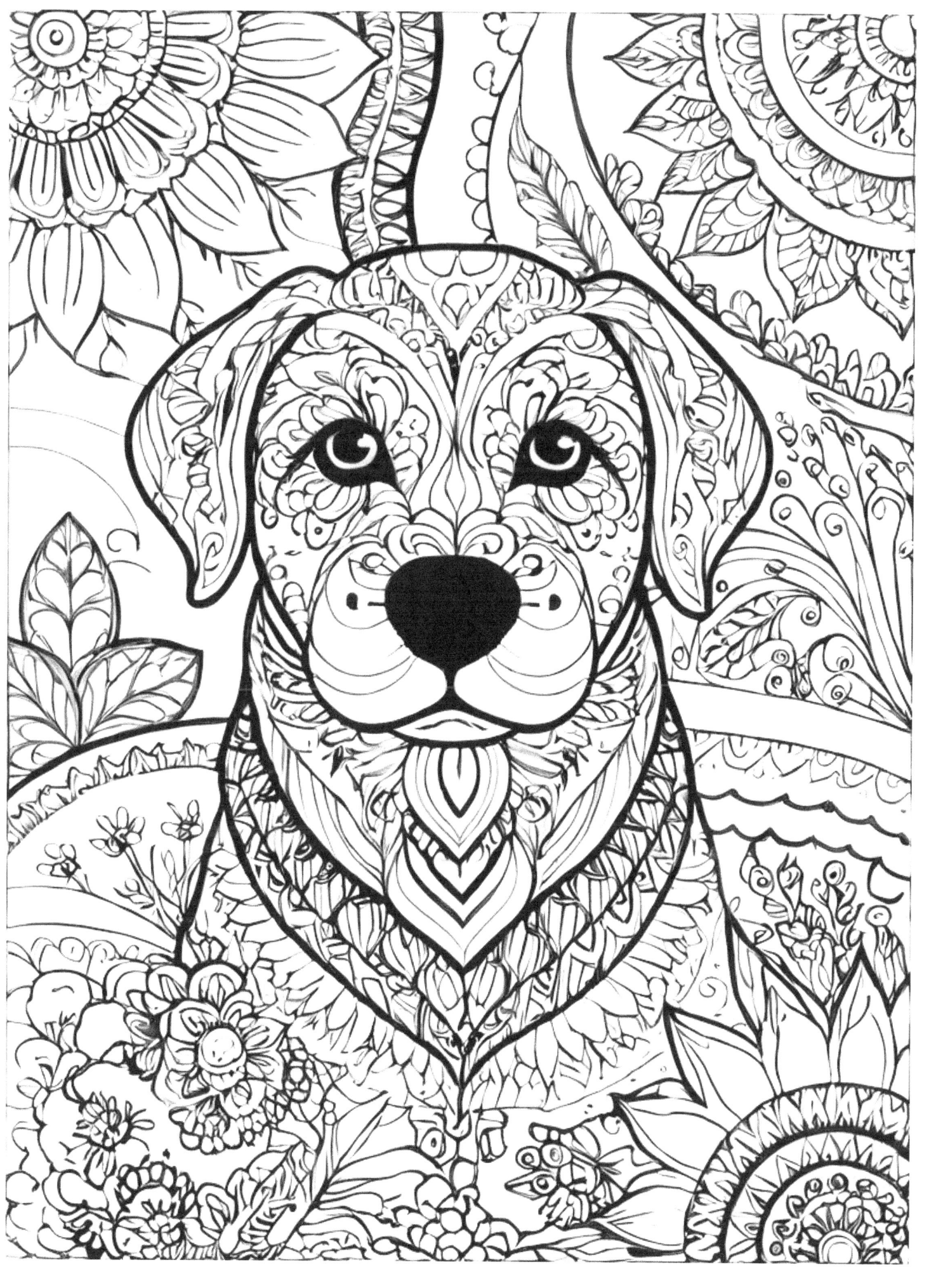

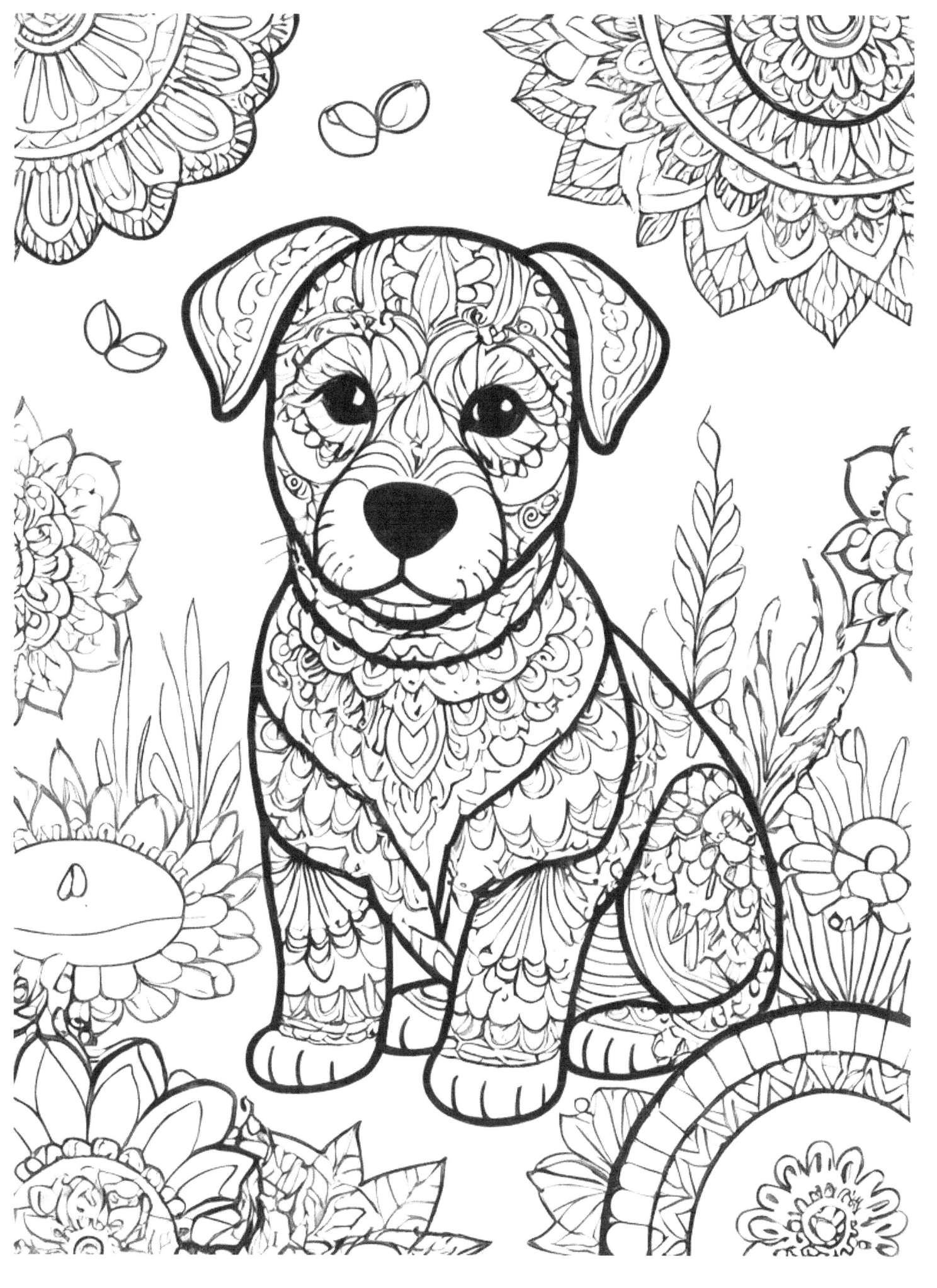